TARGET RIFLE SHOOTING

E. G. B. REYNOLDS
and ROBIN FULTON

BARRIE & JENKINS
COMMUNICA-EUROPA

First published 1972
by
Barrie & Jenkins Ltd
24 Highbury Crescent London N5 1RX

Second Edition 1976

ISBN 0 214 20172 4

Printed and bound in Great Britain by
REDWOOD BURN LIMITED
Trowbridge & Esher

CONTENTS

LIST OF PLATES

ON THE AUTHORS

Major E. G. B. Reynolds

Edward Reynolds served in the first World War in France with the 11th Bn. The Rifle Brigade. In World War Two, he served on the staff of the Sniper Wing of the Small Arms School at Bisley. He was for fourteen years a Technical Officer on Inspectorate of Armaments Headquarters Staff, dealing chiefly with the inspection and development of small arms, in particular, rifles. He was closely concerned with inspection and development of the No. 4 (Lee-Enfield) Rifle.

Rifle shooting has been his principal hobby for over fifty years. Full-bore international honours include Kolapore, National, Mackinnon, World Championship and Britannia Shield Matches. Small-bore international honours include the Dewar Trophy Match (ten times), the Pershing Trophy, the Lord Wakefield, and World Championship Matches (Granada 1933 and Stockholm 1947).

He was the first marksman to make a full score of 400 ex 400 in the Dewar Match, in 1933—a world record; and a British record 300 ex 300 in the Home Countries International Match in 1932.

Other shooting honours include: silver medals, full-bore and small-bore, in the World Championships at Stockholm in 1947, nine times in the Queen's Prize final, several times winner of Suffolk County Championships, and numerous Bisley successes, full-bore and small-bore.

Major Reynolds has also written *The Lee-Enfield Rifle*, a history of a famous weapon from first designs to the present day.

Major R. A. Fulton, T.D.

Robin Fulton represents the third generation of a family that has a unique connection with target rifle shooting. He followed his father into the family gunsmith's business, which was founded by his grandfather in the days when the N.R.A. held its meetings at Wimbledon. All three bear the distinction

9

of having won the King's or Queen's Prize for rifle shooting; Arthur Fulton, the author's father, being the only person to achieve this on three occasions.

During the 1939-45 War, he became a Small Arms Technical Officer, qualifying in this capacity at the Military College of Science. He served for two and a half years with the Australian Army, and was concerned with the development and trial of a wide variety of small arms.

In addition to winning the Queen's Prize in 1958, and being second in 1959, Robin Fulton has nineteen King's or Queen's Hundred badges to his credit. He has won the Duke of Gloucester's Prize, the Grand Aggregate Silver Cross twice, the Daily Mail three times, and many other first prizes including the Canadian Grand Aggregate on two occasions. He has been champion shot of Surrey four times, has represented Great Britain in Empire, Kolapore and Palma Matches, England in National and Mackinnon Matches, and has been in British touring teams to Canada, South Africa, Australia, New Zealand, Rhodesia, and the World Championships in Stockholm in 1947. He was Vice Captain of the G.B. Team to Canada in 1966, Captain of the G.B. Team to Australia and New Zealand in 1968, and more recently captained the G.B. Kolapore Team at Bisley in 1973 and the England National Team in 1975.

AUTHORS' PREFACE

With many years of target shooting experience and a reasonable measure of success behind them, the authors feel that the knowledge they have accumulated may be of some use to their fellow marksmen, especially those who have only recently commenced or are about to commence their target shooting careers.

Such is the nature of target shooting that no hard and fast rules can be laid down which will ensure success. There are many ways of tackling the numerous problems which arise and what is found to suit one person may prove unsuitable for another. There are, however, certain fundamentals which the authors firmly believe should be observed if success is to be achieved and these are explained as fully and simply as possible.

A fascinating aspect of target shooting is that one never ceases to learn, and for this reason it is sincerely hoped that even the most experienced marksmen will find something of value in these pages.

The authors take this opportunity of thanking all those who have so kindly helped them in their endeavours to make the book of real value, especially the late Rear Admiral F. E. P. Hutton C.B. for his Wind Chart and advice, and Ted Molyneux for his voluntary and willing assistance in preparing many of the line drawings. They are also grateful to Lt. Col. T. W. Whittaker O.B.E. (Secretary, Army Rifle Association), Michael Baxter (Chairman, British Sporting Rifle Club) and David Parrish for their knowledgeable advice on shooting under U.I.T. Rules.

FOREWORD

Shooting has been one of man's essential activities from time immemorial. Shooting with the sling and the bow for food and for war was early developed to a high degree of accuracy and effect—we need only to think of the boy David's inspired shot with a stone from a sling; of the Persian arrows at Thermopylae, so dense a cloud that they hid the sun and drew from Leonidas the tremendous (but unavailing) 'So much the better, we shall fight in the shade'; and of the devastating marksmanship of the English bowmen that won the Battle of Crécy. But it was not until the invention of gunpowder, and its application as a propellant by Schwartz and by Roger Bacon in the middle of the 14th century, that firearms entered the scene.

They developed so quickly and so quickly superseded the longbow that by 1590 we find that old soldier Sir John Smythe lamenting that the day of the longbow was over before his time; and not only that, but even the modern firearms were inferior to those of his youth. Yet it was not (as was remarked by Sir Winston Churchill) until after Waterloo that hand firearms developed greater range and greater accuracy, greater penetration and a higher rate of fire than the longbow of Crécy; nor until after Alexander Forsyth's invention of the percussion system and the development of the military breech loading rifle in the 19th century that, as a product of the Volunteer movement of 1859, target shooting with the rifle became a widespread and patriotic pastime.

It is with the most recent manifestations of that long perspective that this book concerns itself, and more particularly with the changes that have led, after a century in which the staple of fullbore shooting in this country and throughout the British Commonwealth was firmly based on the military rifle, to the development and adoption of the Target Rifle for competitive fullbore shooting, no longer using the military rifle (which in its modern selfloading form is unsuitable for precision target shooting) but still using the military cartridge.

It is more than half a century since Ommundsen and Robinson published their great work on *Rifles and Ammunition;* the recent changes have brought new problems and new techniques, and it is good that Major Reynolds and Major Fulton have in this book on *Target Rifle Shooting* now brought the story up to the present day.

None could be better qualified to do so. The authors are both marksmen of great distinction, Major Fulton indeed being unique in having followed his father and his grandfather as a winner of the Queen's Prize; and both are acknowledged experts on the technical aspects of rifles and rifle shooting, Major Reynolds having for his part written the definitive history of the Lee Enfield rifle. It is of great value to all those who enjoy the sport of target shooting with the rifle, or who contemplate doing so, that the fruits of their unsurpassed experience and expertise are set down and made available to us; they deserve the gratitude and the congratulations of us all for this important contribution to the knowledge and understanding of the true doctrines of modern marksmanship.

Cottesloe
25 November 1971

AN HISTORICAL NOTE

Wars and threats of war have left their mark on British target shooting. It was, in fact, the possibility of invasion by the third Napoleon that inspired the creation of the Volunteer Movement and led to a wide appreciation of the rifle both in the framework of National Defence and competitive target shooting.

Target shooting became properly organized with the formation of the National Rifle Association in 1860. The first practical step was to stage a National Prize Meeting, and suitable ranges for this purpose were built on Wimbledon Common. Her Majesty Queen Victoria strongly supported the target shooting movement both actively and financially. She founded an annual prize of £250 for competition among the Volunteers and fired the first shot at the original Meeting at Wimbledon in 1860. Thus was laid the foundation stone of British target shooting which, for many years, was largely confined to the Volunteer Forces and closely followed the trend of musketry training requirements. Plates 1 to 4 show the types of Service rifles which were used at Wimbledon.

Inevitably, due to building development around Wimbledon and the impending introduction of the .303 in. Lee-Metford rifle (plate 5) with its greater range, a move to a less populous area became necessary, and in 1890, after the investigation of a number of possible sites, the N.R.A. moved from Wimbledon to Bisley.

The South African campaign, in which the limitations of British marksmanship were sadly exposed, awakened a more general interest in the rifle throughout Great Britain and the Colonies and the value of accurate shooting received new appreciation. Hitherto, a young man had little opportunity of even handling a rifle unless he belonged to one of the Military Auxiliary organizations. Consequently, many of the newly formed volunteer army who went to South Africa had received little training in the use of the weapon with which they were

THE EARLIEST QUEEN'S PRIZE WINNERS.

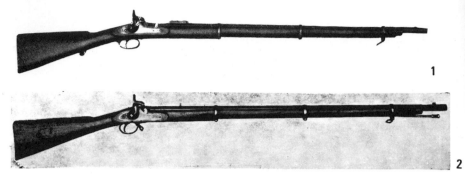

1

2

Plate 1 & 2. The Enfield (top) and the Whitworth were the first rifles to be used in the contest for H.M. the Queen's Prize, inaugurated in 1860. Enfields were used in the first stage but they were not accurate enough for long ranges and Whitworths were used in the final. The Whitworth was a very accurate rifle and dominated the prize lists in the long range events at the early Wimbledon prize meetings.

Plate 3. The Snider-Enfield. The action of the Enfield rifle after conversion to breech-loading. The Snider superseded the muzzle loading Enfield on the ranges at Wimbledon in 1871, and the Queen's Prize was, for the first time, shot throughout with breech-loaders.

3

4

Plate 4. The Martini-Henry. In 1871, Martini-Henry rifles, specially served out to competitors by the War Office, superseded Whitworths in the second (then the final) stage of the Queen's Prize. In 1878, the War Office issued Martini-Henry rifles to competitors in the first stage, and six years later the rifle was in general use in all the Service rifle competitions at Wimbledon.

Plate 5. The Lee-Metford. The Lee-Metford superseded the Martini-Henry, and in 1897 the competitions at Bisley for rifles in the hands of Volunteers became known as 'Service Rifle' competitions.

expected to kill the enemy and protect themselves. In the British Regular Army, competitive target shooting was in its infancy, the Army Rifle Association having been formed only a few years previously.

The war also changed ideas regarding the firing positions which were in general use in target shooting. These had more or less conformed to military requirements; standing, kneeling, and sitting prevailing in the Service Rifle competitions and in general range practice. The prone position was largely confined to the longer distances. In the early months of the South African War, the British troops sustained many casualties through failing adequately to conceal themselves in action. The advantages of the prone position became abundantly evident and, as a consequence, the other firing positions disappeared from competitive shooting other than in a few events primarily for the Armed Forces.

The civilian rifle club movement was stimulated by lessons learned in the Boer War. The desire of civilians to become proficient in the use of the rifle without having to join a military organization was at last appreciated and encouraged. Concessions were granted by the War Office on the purchase cost of Government rifles and ammunition, and club members were exempted from having to hold gun licences. To enjoy these concessions rifle clubs in Great Britain had to affiliate to the National Rifle Association, and a list of all club members had to be sent each year to the General Officer Commanding the District in which the club was located. Thus the military authorities had up-to-date information on target shooting enthusiasts throughout the country for possible use in a national emergency.

Field-Marshal Lord Roberts V.C., who had commanded the British Forces in South Africa, strongly supported a campaign to establish a rifle club in every town and village in Great Britain. Though this objective was never reached, many new clubs were formed, though the stringent safety regulations governing the building of full-bore ranges made it necessary for clubs to come to an arrangement with the military authorities to use the existing Service ranges. Miniature Rifle Clubs (.22 in.) had a much easier range problem and such clubs increased rapidly in both town and rural districts. This led to the formation of the Society of Miniature Rifle Clubs (now the National Small-bore Rifle Association), which relieved the N.R.A. of the organization of competitive .22 in. target shooting.

In 1908, the Territorial Army supplanted the Volunteer Force in Great Britain and a close liaison was established between the County Rifle Associations and their respective County Territorial Associations. The year was also marked by an important innovation, aperture backsights being permitted for use on the Service rifle in competitive shooting. Previously, the use of orthoptic spectacles (figure 1) had been permitted to give

Fig. 1. Orthoptic Spectacles. The forerunner of the aperture sight, used to improve the definition of standard open sights in competition shooting.

better definition in aiming. The frame for the aiming eye in these spectacles was filled with an opaque disc in which there was a small aperture. The effect produced was similar to that of a normal aperture sight, and in fact led to the development and ultimate adoption of such sights. Even though the National Rifle Association and the British War Office were in full agreement on the introduction of the aperture sight as being easier and more accurate to use than 'open' sights, over thirty years elapsed before they were in general use in the British Army. Some early aperture folding sights are illustrated in plates 6 to 10.

The First World War soon showed the value of the civilian rifle club movement. The N.R.A. was authorised by the War Office to form a school of musketry at Bisley Camp to train musketry instructors. The school proved invaluable, and many thousands of instructors were trained and posted to units in all theatres of war. Younger members of the N.R.A. on active service turned their knowledge of target shooting to good purpose as snipers, many of them being seconded to sniping schools as instructors. The N.R.A. report for 1916 included the following: 'Every penny spent by marksmen on Bisley has been an investment towards war needs, for without Bisley there would have been no organization ready to which Lord Kitchener could have turned for aid'.

EARLY APERTURE FOLDING BACKSIGHTS.

Plate 6. The 'nose-knocker' designed to fit in place of the backsight portion of the long range dial sight. In use about 1907.

Plate 7. The B.S.A. sight designed for long Lee-Enfield rifles. **First produced** about 1908.

Plate 8. The B.S.A.-Tippins sight. First used about 1910.

Plate 9. The A. J. Parker model 9.G.

Plate 10. The A. J. Parker model T.Z.

Plate 11. No. 4 rifle action body stiffened by metal plate.

When full-bore target shooting was resumed after hostilities had ceased, all the important competitions at the Bisley Meeting were thrown open to past as well as present members of H.M. Forces of both sexes. This created two distinct classes of Service Rifle marksmen to be catered for; serving members of the British Regular and Auxiliary Forces and the civilian enthusiasts who shot for pleasure. These two classes were known as Service Rifle Class 'A' (S.R.a.) for those who shot under more or less Service conditions, and Service Rifle Class 'B' (S.R.b.) for those who shot as a recreational pastime. In 1968 the N.R.A. Range Regulations were altered to allow any bolt-action rifle approved by the Council to be used in the latter class. The two classes, prevailing to-day, then became S.R.—Service Rifle and T.R.—Target Rifle. The Target Rifle rules govern most of the important competitive fixtures and, as only the prone position is used, people of all ages including many with physical disabilities can take part. It remains the principal form of full-bore target shooting throughout the British Commonwealth.

The 1914-18 War was also responsible for the semi circular (tin-hat) aiming mark, designed to represent a steel-helmeted head appearing over a trench parapet. It was introduced at the 1920 Bisley Meeting for ranges up to 600 yards and was in use until 1969 when it was superseded by a circular black aiming mark similar to that used at the longer ranges.

British and Commonwealth full-bore shooting had now formed a pattern which, apart from equipment, has changed little to-day, except that in the Armed Forces the emphasis is on quick shooting at short distances at fleeting and indistinct targets.

The early 1920's were difficult years for rifle clubs in the United Kingdom. The country was sick of war and everything pertaining to it, and target shooting received a certain amount of unjust criticism as being preparation for war. Conditions of industrial unrest, unemployment and a general shortage of money added to the difficulties. However, most rifle clubs survived and, as war memories faded, a new generation became interested in target shooting as a sport and a steady revival took place. The revival was particularly noticeable in the School Cadet Forces, each succeeding year showing an increase in the number of schools competing at the Bisley Meeting. Target shooting was flourishing when the Second World War put an end to 'shooting for pleasure'.

The early days of Hitler's war showed no immediate requirement for accurate rifle shooting, and it was the German army which first proved the value of trained snipers in a war of movement. Sniping had become almost a lost art in the British Army and so the N.R.A. was again asked to provide instructors to teach marksmanship to potential sniping instructors. The training school became known as the N.R.A. Wing of the Small Arms School, and it did much useful work.

With the end of the Second World War, H.M. King George VI decided to open the competition for the King's Prize—which till then had been restricted to past and present members of the Armed Forces—to all British subjects. This change was also applied to the other principal Bisley competitions.

The pattern of Target Rifle shooting now seems unlikely to change to any great extent. In its present form it provides training in the use and care of arms and a sporting pastime which can be universally enjoyed by both sexes of all ages. Not the least of its assets is that it is a form of target shooting common to marksmen in most of the Commonwealth and many other countries. It is certain that no higher standards of sportsmanship and friendly rivalry exist than those which prevail in the international matches that are regular features of the shooting calendar.

THE RIFLE AND CARTRIDGE AND

MATTERS AFFECTING ACCURACY

THE RIFLE. Probably the simplest definition of a rifle is that it is a handgun fitted with a barrel embodying spiral grooves known as 'rifling'.

The earliest rifles were loaded from the muzzle end by means of a ramrod, and the charge, projectile, wads etc. were inserted separately and rammed home. Their modern counterparts known as breech-loading rifles can be opened at the breech end and the complete cartridge inserted in one operation. Rifles are also classified according to their mechanisms, most modern target weapons being of the breech-loading bolt-actioned type; so called because that part of the breech which opens to admit the cartridge is similar in shape and operation to a door-bolt.

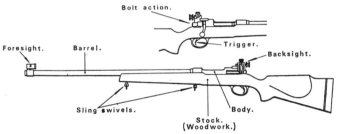

Fig. 2. The principal component parts of a modern target rifle.

The principal component parts of a rifle are the barrel, body (receiver), breech mechanism (action), stock or woodwork and the sighting system (figure 2).

The barrel is a steel tube which may be between 25 and 30 inches in length, in the bore of which are cut the rifling grooves and chamber. The former imparts a spinning motion to the bullet and the chamber houses the cartridge. That part of the bore between the forward end of the chamber and the point at which the rifling is full depth is called the lead (pronounced 'leed') (figure 3). Its purpose is to ensure that the axis of the

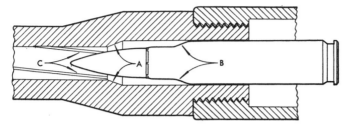

Fig. 3. How a rimless case is positioned in the chamber.
A   The forward part of the chamber (the small cone) which controls the position of the rimless cartridge and the amount of headspace.
B   The shoulders of the cartridge.
C   The lead.

bullet and bore are coincident. An imaginary line running down the centre of the bore is termed 'the axis of the barrel'.

The barrel is screwed or breeched into the forward end of the body which also accommodates the bolt mechanism and magazine (if any) and the whole is firmly anchored to the stock by means of bolts or screws. The body is subjected to considerable stress when a cartridge is fired and it indirectly resists the whole rearward pressure of the exploding charge.

The bolt, which contains the firing mechanism, is locked to the body at the moment of firing. In this position it supports the cartridge in the chamber and seals the breech.

The stock or woodwork gives support to the barrel and action and makes for comfort and convenience when handling the rifle. As the barrel and action body are in contact with the woodwork in most rifles it can have considerable effect on accuracy.

The sighting system consists of a backsight and foresight, the former being capable of adjustment for elevation and lateral correction. The foresight may be in the form of a blade (post) or ring (chapter 7). The distance between the backsight and foresight is known as the sight radius. An imaginary line running through the centre of the backsight and aperture blade foresight tip (or centre of ring) is known as 'the line of sight' (figure 4).

RIFLE AND CARTRIDGE. Some appreciation of what takes place in a rifle when the trigger is pressed and what happens to a bullet after it leaves the barrel, helps towards an understanding of the accuracy limits of rifle and cartridge. It also helps to

Fig. 4.
A   Line of sight.
B   Line of departure of bullet.
C   Trajectory.
Note This drawing is not intended to show a true line of trajectory, which should commence to fall immediately the bullet leaves the muzzle of the rifle.

make clear why certain precautions are necessary if a high standard of accuracy is to be maintained. When a cartridge is fired, the gas from the propellant charge instantly exerts pressure in every direction—on the walls of the chamber, on the face of the bolt-head, and on the base of the bullet. This pressure continues to increase throughout the time the charge is burning, but so rapid is this process that the bullet will have travelled no more than a few inches up the barrel before maximum pressure has been reached. Pressure then begins to decrease; but despite this, the velocity of the bullet continues to accelerate until it leaves the muzzle.

The shock of discharge causes the rifle to recoil, at the same time rotating the weapon about its centre of gravity and producing an upward or downward movement known as 'jump' (figure 5). It also sets up vibrations in the barrel in both the vertical and horizontal planes. Thus the rifle is moving when the bullet emerges from the muzzle. The amount it moves and the consistency of the movement with each cartridge fired are prime factors in determining the accuracy of each individual weapon.

Fig. 5. Movement of the rifle known as 'jump'.
A—B   Axis of bore.
C—D   Direction of muzzle movement.

After the bullet has left the muzzle, the gases in the barrel are free to accelerate, and this results in a further backward force on the rifle. The velocity attained by the acclerating gases from a Service cartridge is about 4,000 feet per second. These gases overtake the bullet and may have some small effect on accuracy. The effect on the rifle is to increase the recoil but, as this takes place after the bullet has left, it cannot affect accuracy.

MATTERS AFFECTING ACCURACY. Many factors contribute to inaccuracy, both before and after the bullet leaves the barrel. Some are inherent in the design and manufacture of weapon and cartridge, but some are the result of the owner's neglect or carelessness and could be avoided.

After the bullet has left the barrel it is subjected to forces that cannot be controlled but, in some cases, their effect can be minimised. Every effort should therefore be taken to ensure consistency in those factors over which it is possible to exercise some measure of control.

EFFECT OF RIFLING. The effect of rifling is to make the bullet spin about its axis and so keep it steady in flight. The speed at which the bullet spins is determined by the twist of the rifling and the force exerted on the base of the bullet by the propellant charge. Without rifling, an elongated projectile, such as a modern rifle bullet, would be completely unstable in flight, turning end over end in its passage through the air. In most target rifles the rifling makes one complete turn in 12 inches. Thus a bullet makes between 2 and 3 revolutions while passing through the barrel and is spinning at about 3,000 revolutions per second when it quits the barrel.

A bullet that enters the rifling in such a manner that it does not spin truly on its axis is unlikely to recover; it will fly unsteadily through the air and will therefore be inaccurate at the target. A flat based bullet is said to 'set up' as it enters the rifling. This means that the base of the bullet expands to fill the rifling grooves as it leaves the neck of the cartridge case, forming a seal against the following gases from the propellant charge. This is known as 'obturation'. Incomplete obturation, causing instability in flight, can result from a deformed bullet but is more likely to be due to a worn bullet lead. Gas getting past a bullet while it is still travelling up the barrel is a common cause of inaccuracy and is due to excessive barrel wear.

Modern streamlined or boat-tailed bullets do not 'set up' in the same way as flat based bullets. They rely for their obturation of the bore on an interference fit with the grooves of the rifling. In the case of the 7.62 mm or 308 in. cartridge, the bullet diameter is .3085 in. (maximum) and the groove diameter of the rifling is .3083 in., with very small manufacturing tolerance.

BARREL VIBRATIONS AND JUMP. Barrel vibrations are not distinct motions but combined elements of a complex movement. They commence immediately the trigger is pressed, caused by the movement of the cocking-piece and striker as they move forward to fire the cartridge. Very rapid vibrations, immediately followed by slower ones, occur at the instant of explosion. An even greater vibration takes effect at the moment the bullet leaves the barrel. All these movements combined determine the direction of the muzzle in relation to the line of sight, and this will vary with any slight differences in the time that the bullet takes to travel the length of the barrel. With the barrel continuously moving from the moment the trigger is pressed until the bullet has left the muzzle, it is unlikely that it will be directed at exactly the same point when the bullet leaves the muzzle as when the trigger is pressed.

The angle formed by the axis of the barrel before the cartridge is fired and the line of departure of the bullet is known as the 'angle of jump'. When a bullet leaves the muzzle with the barrel directed at a higher point than before the round was fired, the rifle is said to have 'positive jump'. When the reverse occurs, the jump is said to be 'negative'. Correction for jump is made in the sighting of the rifle.

INFLUENCES ON BARREL VIBRATIONS (INTERNAL). The bullet fits the bore very tightly and, as the gases from the propellant charge force it towards the muzzle, considerable friction results between bullet and bore. The effect of this is to hold the bullet back and at the same time to drag the weapon forward. As the bullet engages the rifling it tries to make the barrel rotate in the reverse direction to that in which the bullet commences to spin. The internal conditions of the bore can therefore have a considerable influence on accuracy. If rough and corroded, increased friction will occur between bullet and rifling resulting in the build up of metallic and other fouling. Similarly, oil or grease will have a detrimental effect on the first rounds fired.

Cartridges also produce individual variations, but these are mostly beyond the control of the marksman and he can do little about them.

INFLUENCES ON BARREL VIBRATIONS (EXTERNAL). The vibrations are distributed throughout the entire weapon as it recoils, and they must be consistent for every shot for accurate shooting. Consistency largely depends upon even bearings of the locking mechanism and the positions at which the body and barrel bear on the woodwork. Any movement or irregularity at these bearing points, or variations in sling tension, will disturb vibration distribution and adversely affect accuracy.

COMPENSATION. Compensation is the term used to describe the effect of barrel movement in the vertical plane.

The vertical position of the vibrating muzzle when the bullet makes its exit depends on the bullet's travel time in the barrel; and this depends on the bullet's initial velocity and the amount of friction it has to overcome. Variations in these two factors will cause bullets to emerge from the barrel at slightly differing angles of elevation.

A fast bullet leaving the barrel during an upward vibratory movement quits the bore earlier and therefore at a lower point in the barrel's movement than a slower bullet. It also has a flatter trajectory. The point at which the trajectory curves of fast, slow, and medium paced bullets intersect is called the 'compensating range' of the rifle (figure 6). The grouping capacity of any weapon will be better at this distance than at any other as the effect of velocity variation is eliminated.

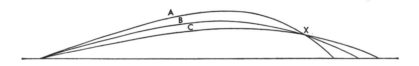

Fig. 6. Compensation.
A   Trajectory of low velocity bullets.
B   Trajectory of medium velocity bullets.
C   Trajectory of high velocity bullets.
X   Point of compensation.

By contrast, the rifle which discharges its bullets during a downward movement will not compensate. The faster bullets will leave the barrel at a higher point than the slower, with the result that the two trajectories move progressively further apart as the range increases. This is known as 'negative compensation'.

A rifle that compensates can only do so at one particular distance, and for this reason some rifles give consistently closer grouping at long ranges than at short, and vice versa.

Whether a rifle has positive or negative compensation is determined by firing specially loaded cartridges. Usually two batches are prepared—one containing plus one grain of propellant and the other minus one grain (above and below the normal standard charge). The cartridge cases of these special rounds are marked '+' and '—' to avoid confusion. Firing is conducted at 25 yards. A small number of normal load cartridges are fired to establish the mean point of impact (m.p.i.), and these are followed by two or three 'plus' and a similar number of 'minus' rounds. If the 'plus' bullets form a group below the normal and the 'minus' above, it can be assumed that the weapon has positive compensation. If the converse occurs, the compensation is negative. The distance apart of the 'plus' and 'minus' groups will give a rough guide as to the compensating range. If very widely apart, the possibility is that the compensating range will be at the longer distances, and vice versa. If there is no difference in group position between the normal and the 'plus' and 'minus' cartridges, the rifle can be assumed to have no compensating range and will probably be extremely good at short ranges though probably more susceptible to velocity variations at longer distances.

GRAVITY. As the bullet leaves the muzzle it is immediately influenced by the force of gravity. It is therefore evident that a bullet must be directed as much above the object it is intended to hit as the amout it will be forced downwards by gravity on its journey. The muzzle of the barrel must be elevated, and the angle formed by the axis of the barrel with the line of sight is known as the 'angle of tangent elevation'.

The action of a bullet emerging from a barrel is rather like that of a jet of water from the nozzle of a garden hose. The water shoots forth, its angle of arc dependent on the angle at which the nozzle is elevated, its trajectory dependent on the force behind the water. The stronger the jet the flatter will be its trajectory. A bullet in flight behaves in exactly the same way, never actually travelling in a straight line but falling at a rate of acceleration of 32.19 feet per second per second.

If gravity were the only force acting on it, the bullet's flight would be in the form of a parabola (figure 7). Its maximum range would then be obtained with the barrel at an angle of tangent elevation of 45 degrees. It is estimated that a normal Service rifle bullet would, under these conditions, travel a distance of about 35 miles. Gravity, however, is not the only force to be reckoned with. A second force—and more difficult to resolve because it is highly variable—is the resistance of the air.

AIR RESISTANCE. The atmosphere offers resistance to any solid object attempting to pass through it; and the resistance varies

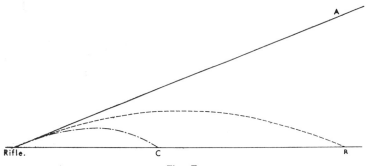

Fig. 7.
A Unimpeded flight.
B Gravity only affecting flight.
C Gravity and air resistance affecting flight.

according to the density of the atmosphere and the size, weight, shape, and speed of the object. Atmospheric resistance acts as a brake, and the faster the bullet's speed the greater the resistance of the air through which it passes. The instant the bullet moves it has to displace the air in front of it. To do this it must employ force, and force used is force expended. Speed decreases at once, and the further the bullet travels the higher will be the rate of diminution. The slower the bullet travels the steeper is its angle of descent (figure 6).

VARIATIONS IN AIR RESISTANCE. Density of atmosphere varies at different elevations above sea level. It also varies with the humidity and temperature of the air. The denser the atmosphere, the greater resistance it offers to a moving body. In the United Kingdom, normal conditions are assumed to be:
   Barometric pressure—30 inches.
   Thermometer reading—60 degrees Fahrenheit.
Barometric changes are of less importance than changes of temperature, which can be rapid and considerable. The following elevation adjustments can be regarded as a good general rule and near enough correct for all practical purposes:
   (a) For every inch the barometer rises above or falls below 30 inches, add or deduct 1½ yards per 100 yards of range.
   (b) For every 10 degrees the thermometer rises above or falls below 60 degrees Fahrenheit, add or deduct 1 yard per 100 yards of range.
Thus a fall of one inch on the barometer has the same effect as a rise of fifteen degrees on the thermometer.

For example, if when shooting at 500 yards the barometer falls 1½ inches—temperature remaining constant—the resultant decrease in air resistance will have the effect of increasing the distance travelled by the bullet by 10 yards, so the backsight would have to be lowered appropriately. A similar effect will follow a rise in the thermometer of 20 degrees F.—barometric pressure remaining constant. In theory the backsight would need lowering by a little over ½ minute at 500 yards and approximately 2 minutes at 1,000 yards to counteract these effects.

A rifle zeroed at sea level would, if fired at an altitude of 4,000 feet, require approximately 10% less elevation to hit the target at 1,000 yards. In Rhodesia, rapid changes in temperature of 30 to 40 degrees are common. On the Salisbury Rifle Range, which is approximately 4,700 feet above sea level, the normal barometric pressure is just over 25 inches against sea level pressure of about 29½ inches. On this range, normal elevations are ½ minute less at 300 yards, 2 minutes less at 600 yards, and 4½ minutes less at 1,000 yards than in the United Kingdom, where elevation adjustments caused by changes of atmospheric density are of significance only at ranges of 900 yards and beyond; they are seldom taken into consideration at the shorter distances.

A simple rule—and near enough for all practical purposes— is that a change of 1 inch barometric, or 15 degrees F. in temperature, will require a change in elevation of about ½ minute at 600 yards and 1½ minutes at 1,000 yards.

DRIFT AND YAW. Drift is the lateral deviation of a bullet from its course after it leaves the rifle, and is caused by the spin of the bullet and air resistance. Over the past hundred years many explanations of drift have been expounded and there is still no definite proof of exactly what takes place, though there are certain established facts. It is known that projectiles having rounded or pointed heads drift to the left when fired from left-handed rifling and to the right from right-handed rifling. The sharper the twist of the rifling the greater will be the amount of drift. At short ranges, where the trajectory is comparatively flat, drift is practically negligible. Conversely, at extreme ranges, where the trajectory curve is great, and the velocity of the projectile is quickly diminishing, drift is considerable.

When a bullet is fired at a distant object, the axis of the barrel is directed at a point above that object, and the bullet starts its flight on the line of projection (figure 7). The tendency is for the axis of the bullet to keep to its original direction and, as the

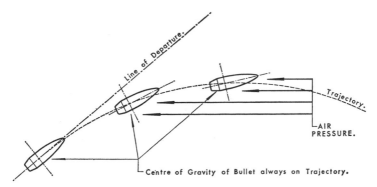

Fig. 8. Drift. The axis of the bullet gets slightly above the line of trajectory. This is known as 'yaw'.

trajectory immediately commences to fall, the nose of the bullet tends to remain slightly above the trajectory (figure 8). This departure of the bullet's spinning axis from the actual trajectory curve is known as 'yaw'. It is gyroscopic in nature, and it tends to increase as the velocity of the projectile decreases and the curvature of the trajectory becomes greater. In other words, the bullet ceases to 'follow its nose', though the spin imparted by the rifling reduces the disruptive effect on accuracy. Figure 8 gives an impression of yaw, showing the angle that the bullet makes to its line of flight.

As a result of this departure of the bullet's axis from its true path, air resistance, instead of being received straight on the point of the bullet, is directed as shown in figure 8. While its general direction is maintained, the point of the bullet develops a tendancy to 'precess' around the trajectory in much the same way as the spinning top (figure 9) moves around the line B-C. This movement—the result of the combined effect of bullet rotation, yaw, and the indirect air resistance—resolves itself into a uniform lateral accleration or 'drift' in the direction in which the bullet is spinning, i.e. to the left from left-handed rifling and to the right from right-handed rifling.

The amount of drift of a .303 Mark 7 bullet fired from a normal Service type barrel is about 10 inches to the left at 1,000 yards i.e. approximately 1 minute of angle. A 7.62 mm bullet will drift by about the same amount and, from a target rifle with right-hand twist rifling, the drift will be to the right. This factor should be borne in mind when zeroing a rifle for long range shooting.

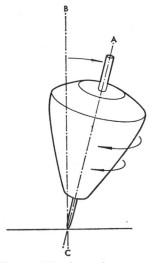

Fig. 9. A spinning top acts in much the same way as a projectile from a rifled firearm. The top is shown as spinning in a clockwise direction. There is a tendency, due to the force of gravity and as a result of retardation, for the top to fall on its side in the direction of the arrow from B to A. In fact, this does not happen as gyroscopic action causes the top to rotate slowly (to precess) about the vertical axis B—C in the same direction as it is spinning. If the illustration is turned on its side, the similarity in behaviour between the spinning top and a bullet in flight becomes obvious.

WIND. Moving air currents, normally referred to as 'wind', affect the flight of a bullet. Measures can be taken to counter this effect and these are fully dealt with in Chapter 11.

BULLET SHAPE AND EFFECT ON ACCURACY. Reference is made in chapter 6 to flat-based and streamlined (boat-tailed) bullets.

When a bullet flies through the air it is accompanied by shock waves, and is followed by a vacuum which causes considerable turbulence as the air closes in behind it. This turbulence has a retarding effect on a bullet and is known as 'drag'. The larger the cross-sectional area of a bullet the greater will be the drag and its consequent retarding effect. The streamlined bullet is designed to lessen the drag by reducing the cross-sectional area of the base of the bullet. Thus, a streamlined bullet will maintain its velocity for a much longer period than a flat-based bullet and, because of its shape, the yaw which develops as it loses velocity is less. A streamlined bullet has a flatter trajectory and is less susceptible to wind effect at long ranges.

3

TARGET RIFLES

RIFLES. For nearly 80 years the .303 in. Lee Enfield Rifle—in one of its various forms—has been the principal weapon used throughout the Commonwealth for competitive target shooting. An exception to this generalisation was the Patt. 14 Enfield Rifle—a modified Mauser design—introduced in 1935. All these were Service Rifles, with little permissible deviation from the standard Military weapon. Certain concessions were allowed in what was known as S.R. (b) (Service Rifle Class 'B') competitions. These took the form of reasonably robust aperture backsights and limited modifications to the 'bedding', or internal adjustment of the rifle, with the object of improving accuracy and making it more suitable for competitive target shooting. In all other respects it remained a Service Rifle.

In 1968, S.R. (b) was superseded by the Target Rifle class, which permits the use of any bolt-actioned rifle—not necessarily of Service design—within certain limits. The restrictions on this class are:

a. Must be readily available in quantity.
b. Must not exceed 5.25 kg (11.64 lb.) in weight including sling.
c. Must fire the standard 7.62 mm NATO cartridge.
d. Trigger pull must not be lighter than 1.5 kg (3.307 lb.), weighed with rifle in vertical position.

With the 7.62 mm cartridge in general use throughout the world, the advent of the target rifle class opened up stimulating possibilities for international shooting. No longer are British full-bore shooters restricted to standard Military rifles and often indifferent Service ammunition.

In 1964, the Dominion of Canada Rifle Association approved the use of No. 4 Rifles modified to take the 7.62 mm cartridge by fitting a suitable barrel of the conventional, i.e. Service, external shape and weight. In all other respects the rifle was unaltered. The results of this initial attempt at conversion for target shooting purposes were rather disappointing as converted rifles and Canadian Service cartridges gave indifferent results, especially at the shorter ranges. Accuracy tended to improve as the range increased and at the longer distances was very good, better even than .303 in. This was in fact a repetition of what happened immediately following World War I when the Short Magazine Lee-Enfield Rifle and the .303 in. Mark 7 cartridge were first used for competition shooting.

The Lee-Enfield Rifle was originally made to fire the .303 in. Mark 6 cartridge which had a 215 grain bullet and a muzzle velocity of approximately 2,100 ft/second. Excellent results were obtained with this combination in the years which culminated in the outbreak of war in 1914. When competitive target shooting was resumed in 1919 the S.M.L.E. Mark 3 Rifle and the Mark 7 cartridge had superseded the earlier types. The latter had a 174 grain bullet and muzzle velocity of approximately 2,400 ft/sec. Largely due to the light, whippy barrel and rather weak action of the S.M.L.E., this combination gave very pronounced positive compensation (chapter 2) and results similar to those obtained in Canada with the 7.62 mm cartridge about forty-five years later.

Whilst the S.M.L.E. rifle could be made to shoot well by the use of 'packing' materials to control the barrel vibrations and reduce the compensating range, the stiffer barrel and action of the No. 4 Rifle did not readily respond to similar treatment. In Canada, strenuous efforts were made and all restrictions removed and, though partially successful, results were not generally considered satisfactory.

Two modifications gave promise of improving short range accuracy. In Australia it was found that by reducing the barrel length to about 21 inches and re-fitting the foresight, improved short range accuracy was obtained. This process undoubtedly caused some loss of velocity and probably reduced it to approximately the same as that of .303 in. ammunition, with similar effect on the rifle's compensation. The other modification was that of stiffening the action body by brazing a metal plate along the top (plate 11). A limited number of trials indicated that the compensating range of rifles so treated was around 600 yards instead of between 1,200 and 1,400 yards as with un-stiffened actions.

At this formative stage, investigations were proceeding to find out what other countries were doing for target shooting with the 7.62 mm Nato round, and the first rifle to be introduced in the United Kingdom from the Continent was the Norwegian Kongsberg Mauser rifle (plate 12). This is a Military style

TARGET RIFLES.

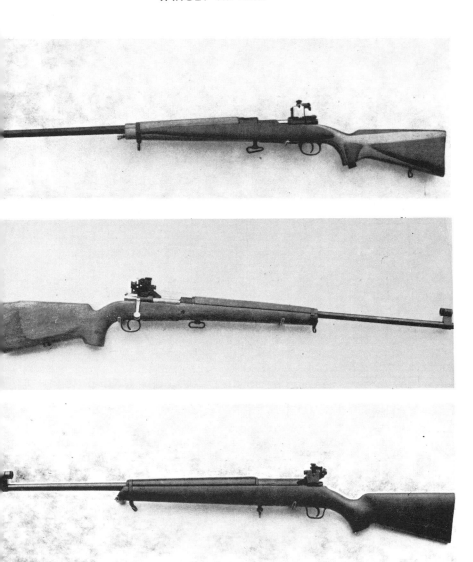

Plate 12.
Top 7.62 mm Kongsberg target rifle, built on Mauser '98 action. Laminated beech/walnut stock.
Centre 7.62 mm Carl Gustav 63 E target rifle Parker-Hale sights.
Bottom 7.62 mm Australian Sportco target rifle. Parker-Hale sights.

weapon originally intended as a sniping rifle and used as such by the Norwegian armed forces. It has become popular with civilian marksmen in Norway for competitive target shooting. A few barrels were also imported and two were re-threaded and fitted to British No. 4 rifles, the woodwork being shortened and modified appropriately. These gave promising results and led to further investigations. Soon, the Danish Schultz & Larsen Mauser and the Swedish Carl Gustav M.63 rifles were undergoing practical trials at Bisley. Meanwhile the Royal Small Arms Factory at Enfield became aware of the situation and investigated the manufacture of heavy barrels for target shooting. By 1968 they had produced sample barrels for Lee-Enfield and Mauser actions which proved very successful. More recently new rifles, specially designed for target shooting with the 7.62 mm cartridge, have been produced by manufacturers in U.K., Australia, Switzerland and Austria (see plates 12 to 15). The wide assortment of rifles, barrels and stock styles, all of which have their good features, presents a perplexing situation to the intending purchaser.

TARGET RIFLE BARRELS. The barrel is probably the most important part of a target rifle, particularly with the modern streamlined or boat-tailed bullets in general use. The older type of flat-based bullet, because of its considerable 'set up', (chapter 2), was not as sensitive to bore imperfections, as already explained. This was particularly true with cartridges containing double-based propellants (chapter 6). The critical relationship between bullet and bore (See chapter 2) makes the dimensioning of the bore, chamber, etc, of extreme importance and small imperfections which were often ignored when flat-based bullets were in general use are now vital to accuracy.

RIFLING. Most Continental barrel makers favour four narrow lands, which necessitate wide grooves. This practice is followed in Australia, Canada and in the United Kingdom, with the exception of the British Self-loading Service rifle which has six-grooved rifling. Some American manufacturers favour five grooves; lands and grooves being of approximately equal width. The diameter across the grooves is the critical factor and most barrels made to take the 7.62 mm Service cartridge are rather tighter in this dimension than those designed for the heavier bullets such as the American National Match or the special heavy-bulleted cartridges used in Match Rifle shooting at Bisley. Some degree of interference fit (chapter 2) between bullet

TARGET RIFLES.

Plate 13.
Top P.14 converted to 7.62 mm, utilizing standard military woodwork. Schultz & Larsen barrel.
Centre 7.62 mm Musgrave (R.S.A.) Target Rifle.
Bottom Fulton custom-built Mauser. American walnut stock and Schultz & Larsen 7.62 mm barrel.

and bore is essential for a high degree of accuracy with cartridges which have not been manufactured with target shooting accuracy as the main objective.

With bullets whose nominal diameter is .308 in. minimum, and weight in the region of 170-180 grains, the best results have been obtained through barrels having a groove diameter not exceeding .3083 in. and a maximum bore diameter of .3005 in. With Service NATO type 144 grain bullets (with short parallel section) successful results have been obtained from barrels having groove diameters as small as .305 in. and bore diameters of .2975 in. It also seems beneficial if the bore is slightly tapered towards the muzzle.

Twist of Rifling. This has recently become a very controversial subject. In theory, the longer the bullet, the steeper should be the pitch of rifling. Thus, the .303 in. 174 grain bullet was considered to be suited to rifling that had one complete turn in 10 inches, and this was equally successful with the Long Lee-Enfield Rifle with its longer 215 grain bullet.

Some of the earlier 7.62 mm barrels introduced in 1969-70 were made with 1 in 10 rifling. Others had 1 in 12. There was some evidence that the latter gave the better results with the rather indifferent Service ammunition used in those first years. With better quality imported ammunition, their performance was admirable. Experiments were later conducted with 1 in 14 twist rifling, and excellent results obtained with barrels so made. The theory behind this is that if a bullet is going to develop a 'yaw' due to imperfection in manufacture, the faster it spins, the greater will be the effect of the yaw. Therefore, provided stability is not affected, a slower rate of spin will reduce this effect. All this is highly theoretical and lacks proof, but it is reasonable to say that the highly sensitive NATO bullet, which is far too short in relation to its diameter to be regarded as a sound ballistic proposition, will give excellent results with both 12 and 14 inch twist rifling provided that the ammunition is of good quality and does not contain too many of the manufacturing defects that can affect accuracy. It is quite certain that external factors cannot improve the accuracy of the ammunition, but they can be so arranged as to make the best of the situation and not aggravate it.

BARREL MANUFACTURE. In recent years considerable progress has been made in the methods of rifling barrels. The conventional method consists of each groove being separately cut by a rifling cutter. This is drawn through the bore a number of

TARGET RIFLES.

Plate 14.
Top P.14 rifle, fitted with Bishop stock and Kongsberg 7.62 mm barrel.
Centre Grunig Elmiger U.I.T. Standard Rifle.
Bottom Model '98 Mauser with Anschutz style stock and handstop.

times, the barrel being rotated after each cut to give the required number of grooves. The cutter is moved spirally in order to produce the appropriate twist or pitch of the rifling. Obviously, this somewhat complicated procedure requires continual supervision and inspection to ensure regularity and perfection, and each barrel has to be lapped or polished afterwards.

Button rifling is a popular, relatively inexpensive, and extremely efficient method, much favoured in America. It consists of forcing a tungsten-carbide rifled 'button'—rather like a round-nosed bullet—through the bore by a hydraulic ram system. This is similar, though simpler, to the broaching method used during World War 2 in Canada. It also has the advantage that there is no limit to the type of rifling, number and depth of grooves, twist etc., that can be produced simply by making a suitable button.

Hammering, or cold swaging, is another method of rifling which has found favour on the Continent and in the United Kingdom (plate 16). This consists of introducing a rifled mandrel into the barrel blank which is then hammered at a very high rate. The external profile is formed by the hammering process and the rifling by the mandrel passing through the bore. This method produces high quality barrels of considerable regularity and has a similar advantage to the button rifling process in that any form of rifling can be incorporated by the relatively simple operation of making a suitable mandrel. The internal finish of hammered barrels is extremely good and no further lapping is necessary. Some degree of 'work-hardening' occurs both externally and internally though opinions differ as to whether this has any effect on barrel life. Theoretically it should prolong it to some extent. The external surface of a hammered barrel is finely patterned with the hammer blows which vary in pattern and uniformity. Some manufacturers turn the exterior of the barrel to give it a smooth finish and to obtain the profile required. Others, depending to some extent upon the type of hammering machine in use, leave the exterior with its hammered finish.

As a generalisation, it can be said that barrels of European manufacture expressly designed for use with the NATO cartridge are likely to give better results with that cartridge than barrels of American manufacture. Though excellent from all points of view, the latter are generally designed with slightly larger bores and less tight rifling grooves and are therefore more suited to the heavier 'match' type bullets favoured in the United States. In any case, most target shooting in America is done with

TARGET RIFLES.

Plate 15.

Top No. 4 conversion (Fulton) with broad target style fore-end, 'Monte Carlo' butt and handstop. Fitted with Ferlach barrel and 7.62 mm magazine.
Centre 7.62 mm Parker-Hale 1200 TX target rifle, built on commercially made Mauser action. Walnut stock.
Bottom Steyr Mannlicher 7.62 mm Target Rifle.

hand-loaded cartridges or with the National Match cartridge which has a 175 grain bullet. Consequently it is difficult to make a direct comparison with European procedure. Conversely, there is some evidence that the tighter European made barrels perform very satisfactorily with the heavy bullet cartridges.

THE CHAMBER AND LEAD (PRONOUNCED 'LEED'). The barrel chamber is of almost equal importance to accuracy as the rifling, as it governs the angle at which the bullet is presented to the rifling. Traditionally, military rifle barrel chambers have been made rather loose and with a greater taper than the cartridge for which they have been designed. This is supposed to assist extraction, particularly in machine-guns as, immediately the cartridge case is withdrawn the smallest amount, it is free from restraint and is easily extracted. Such chambering techniques were adopted in the first 7.62 mm target rifle barrels made at Enfield and the results obtained were perhaps not as good as they should have been. However, this defect was quickly rectified and all barrels from this source are now produced in accord with the most advanced American and Continental techniques, with the result that the bullet is correctly presented to the rifling.

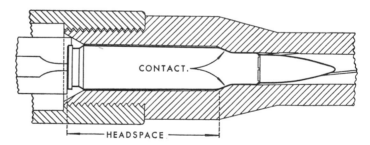

Fig. 10. Headspace (chamber depth). Headspace in modern target rifles firing rimless cartridges. The distances between the bolt face and the shoulders of the chamber.

Another important factor affecting accuracy is the chamber depth, i.e. the distance from the bolt face to a datum line drawn through the shoulder of the chamber (figure 10). This dimension takes the place of headspace, i.e. the distance between the bolt face and the breech face in chambers made for rimmed cartridges. Chamber depth is of considerable consequence and in manufacture is carefully gauged. A tolerance not exceeding .003

in. being permitted between the high and low limits. Here again, there are differences of opinion as to the desirable degree of crush or squeeze on the cartridge when closing the breech. It is the considered opinion of the authors that a very small amount of crush is beneficial as each cartridge is thus 'sized' to suit the chamber. Too much crush is undesirable and a too deep chamber can, in extreme cases, cause a misfire.

The bullet 'lead'—termed 'throat' in the U.S.A.—is of vital importance. As mentioned in chapter 2, it is the short tapered cone between the mouth of the chamber and the point at which the rifling reaches its maximum depth. It is where the bullet lies in the barrel before being fired and, ideally, should be a snug fit and touch the bullet without marking it; thus ensuring that the bullet begins to engage the rifling immediately its forward movement commences. In fact, manufacturing tolerances and permissible variation in cartridge dimensions render this ideal practically impossible. Instances have occured when the lead was so short that the bullet engaged the rifling on closing the bolt. In this condition, if the cartridge is extracted without firing, the bullet may remain stuck in the rifling while the case is withdrawn and the propellant charge strewn into the action, making it necessary for the action to be thoroughly cleaned before further use. A long 'lead' is far more detrimental to accuracy as it allows the bullet a degree of free travel before it engages the rifling, with the result that it may do so at a slight angle. A bullet which does this becomes slightly deformed and will leave the muzzle with a small initial 'yaw' which, inevitably, will get worse the further it travels.

A method of determining whether the lead suits the cartridge is to take out the propellant from the cartridge after removing the bullet by means of an inertia bullet puller. The cap should then be struck as a further precautionary measure and the bullet replaced in the mouth of the case but not pushed fully home. The cartridge should then be fed into the chamber and the bolt carefully and firmly closed. If by this action the bullet is pushed home to its correct position in the cartridge case it can be assumed that the lead in that particular barrel is correct. If the bullet still projects considerably, the lead is too long, and the chamber requires re-cutting and the barrel face turned back to allow for re-breeching.

Certain types of rifle, notably the British No. 4 and the Australian Sportco, have interchangeable bolt-heads which enable the chamber depth to be adjusted easily and effectively. The Mauser type of action with its fixed bolt face presents a more complex problem. Each chamber has to be carefully reamed with a fully profiled reamer to suit the bolt and action to which it is being fitted. Alternatively, the chamber is made to maximum depth and the barrel face and shoulder are turned back to give the actual depth required by the rifle to which it is being fitted.

An interesting departure from the conventional methods has been developed by the Royal Small Arms Factory at Enfield who have introduced a range of breeching washers (plate 17). These are carefully manufactured hardened rings of various thicknesses which are placed between the breeching surfaces of the barrel and action, thus regulating the distance the barrel is screwed into the action (plate 18). By selecting the appropriate washer to suit a barrel and action the correct chamber depth is obtained without reaming. Yet another method achieving the same result is that used in the Kongsberg P.14 barrel. This has a threaded collar which can be positioned as desired, and locked in position to make a 'false' breeching shoulder to suit the action to which it is being fitted. Plate 19 shows some re-barrelling equipment etc.

RIFLE ACTIONS. The only restriction under N.R.A. rules on the type of action used for target rifle construction is that they must be bolt operated. Although this appears to open the door to a very wide variety of rifles, the field is inevitably limited by the supply of suitable barrels. It is not an economical proposition to manufacture barrels threaded for a large selection of actions. Similarly, to screw-cut for individual actions is not a worthwhile proposition for the practising gunsmith and so inevitably a certain amount of uniformity has resulted. This is not a bad thing, as fundamentally rifle shooting is a test of individual skill rather than a test of complex and expensive equipment.

Probably the most popular action in Europe is the German Mauser '98 (figure 11). This is a solidly constructed military front-locking design which has been adapted, modified, copied and employed with considerable success by half the armies in the world. Supplies of this action ex military stocks are generally available, and they are also currently being manufactured on the Continent, primarily for use in sporting rifles and more recently for target rifles. The standard military Mauser has a rather clumsy bolt which sticks out at right-angles to the action. This feature can be effectively modified by setting down the bolt handle in a graceful curve. This gives the necessary clearance for the aperture backsight and is better suited for the target shooter

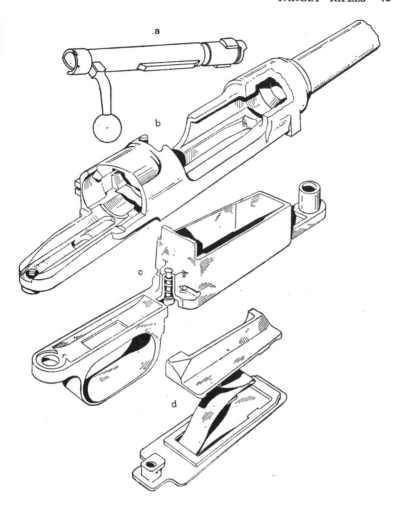

Fig. 11. Mauser action.
A Bolt.
B Action body (receiver).
C Magazine body and trigger-guard.
D Magazine platform, spring and plate.

(plate 21). The Mauser is a forward locking action, i.e. the locking lugs are on the front end of the bolt and lock into recesses in the action body; a third lug is situated at the rear of the bolt.

The standard Mauser '98 action has a 5-round magazine

which is normally left in situ. when used as a target rifle, though it can be omitted if desired and the stock left solid at this point. There is no evidence to indicate that this has any effect on accuracy.

The bearing surfaces on the underside of the action body are flat and symmetrical and lend themselves readily to 'bedding' in the rifle stock. The rear tang is rather long and consequently a weak feature, but there is little evidence to indicate that this adversely affects accuracy. Recoil is taken on a transverse rib under the forward end of the action body which is secured by strong front and rear trigger-guard screws. An adaptor to take the aperture backsight is easily fitted to the rear 'saddle' of the action. This usually consists of an L-shaped bracket secured by two, three or four screws, to the side of which the sight is firmly fixed (plate 20).

The P.'14 and M.'17 rifles are variants of the Mauser theme and embody practically all the Mauser features. They have one or two built-in advantages in that the bolt is already set down in such a way as to make the fitting of an aperture backsight a simple matter. Commercial sights have been available for this type of rifle since 1935 and can be easily fitted by means of a single screw. In addition, the rear tang is much more solid and, in the opinion of American experts, it is considered slightly superior to the normal Mauser—not because of better accuracy but for its ready adaptability for target shooting.

Both the P.'14/M.'17 and Mauser '98 have reasonably good trigger mechanisms but, because of the large number in general use, excellent commercially made adjustable trigger mechanisms —one and two-stage—are available and relatively simple to fit and adjust.

Another Mauser action, much favoured in Sweden, is the M '96 or 'small ring' Mauser. This is basically similar to the M '98 but has a slightly smaller diameter action body (approximately 1.30 inches, the M '98 being 1.40 inches). This action will not take the same barrel as the M '98 which, to some extent, limits its use. It can be fitted with the Swedish Carl Gustav barrel.

A popular rifle which has proved itself readily adaptable to the N.R.A. requirements is the British No. 4 Lee-Enfield (figure 12), which has been a good friend to riflemen in the United Kingdom and the Commonwealth during and since the second world war. As explained earlier, conventional conversion of the No. 4 did not prove successful for target shooting but, when fitted with a 4 lb. target barrel and suitably modified woodwork,

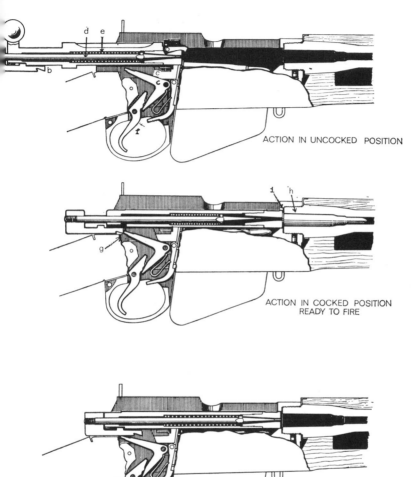

ACTION IN UNCOCKED POSITION

ACTION IN COCKED POSITION
READY TO FIRE

ACTION IN NORMAL POSITION

Fig. 12. How the No. 4 Lee-Enfield action works.

A Cocking-piece.
B Bent.
C Sear.
D Striker.
E Mainspring.

F Trigger.
G Nose of sear engaging bent.
H Cartridge in chamber.
I Headspace.

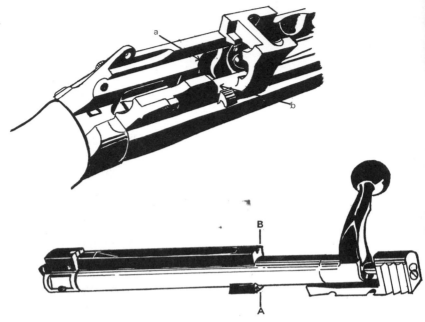

Fig. 13. Method of bolt and body locking in Lee-Enfield rifles.
A   Lug on left side of bolt engages in recess of body (a).
B   Rib on right side of bolt engages resistance shoulder (b).

it becomes a target rifle of high performance. With good quality ammunition—essential with all target weapons—it will hold its own with most other rifles, and at the longer ranges is practically unbeatable. In contrast to the Mauser, the locking lugs are at the rear of the bolt, approximately 4 inches behind the breech face, and consequently there is considerable stretch or spring in the action as it absorbs recoil (figure 13). This is not of great consequence except that it results in very pronounced positive 'compensation'. With other than perfect ammunition this can be a valuable attribute, especially at the longer ranges (See chapter 2 on 'Compensation'). Stiffening the action by brazing a plate on top (already referred to) does not seem to make much difference to compensating characteristics, though some rifles so treated do give good shooting at the shorter distances.

Examples of non-military bolt action rifles that have been produced expressly for the target shooter are becoming more numerous. One of the earlier examples is the now well known Australian Sportco (plate 12).

Another rifle which has been in considerable use at Bisley and elsewhere is the Grunig & Elmiger U.I.T. rifle (plate 14). This is equally applicable to Target Rifle conditions under N.R.A. rules and is used by a minority who like its specialised style of stock. This again has a round action of considerable strength. The bolt has two forward-locking lugs and short striker travel. The bolt face is fully recessed to take the head of the cartridge.

The Steyr-Mannlicher (plate 15) is another new arrival on the scene, one of its distinctive features being that it has a transverse recoil lug or rib at the back of the action instead of in front. The barrel, instead of being threaded into the action body, is fitted by 'shrinking'. By this method, the action body is expanded by heat to take the barrel which is slightly larger than the recess into which it fits, and when cooled the action contracts gripping the barrel firmly. The main objection to this is that it precludes the fitting of other types of barrel, and replacements have to be factory fitted. Inevitably a lengthy and somewhat expensive process.

The Musgrave R.S.A. rifle (plate 13) is yet another purpose made target rifle. This again has a very strong action with solid floor. The underneath bearing surface is flat which is regarded as an advantage when bedding. The barrel is rather shorter (26 ins.) than the majority of contemporary target rifles, but apart from increasing the effect of the nominal 'minute' on backsight adjustment does not seem to have any adverse effect. It is possible to replace the standard barrel with others suitably threaded if desired, and good results have been obtained with rifles so fitted.

This is a simple round-action design with triple front-locking lugs which, in contrast to all other actions, lock directly into special recesses in the barrel. Striker travel is extremely short and the action is provided with a single-stage adjustable trigger mechanism. The recoil shoulder takes the form of a plate between the breeching surfaces of barrel and action and presumably can be used in the same way as the Enfield breeching washers; plates of varying thickness being used to ensure correct breeching-up.

TARGET RIFLE STOCKS. In addition to permitting a variety of barrels more conducive to accuracy than in the past, considerable opportunities are now available for the stock maker to exercise his imaginative skill. Most shooters tend to be conservative in outlook and do not enthuse over elaborate or fancy stocks, but undoubtedly a well designed target stock, carefully fitted to the individual, to obtain maximum comfort while shooting, is a definite asset. There are, of course, a number of marksmen who have shot with Service type rifles all their lives and who do not care for any radical change to weapons of unfamiliar shape and feel. This presents no problem as Service stocks can be modified without difficulty and several target rifles currently available are essentially 'Military' in appearance and styling.

The conventional target stock is one-piece and lends itself to such actions as the Mauser types. The butt has a high straight comb and cheek-piece and is generally fitted with a full pistol grip. Rubber butt pads are usually fitted, and they should be thin and hard. Their purpose is to stop the butt from slipping, not to absorb recoil. The thick ventilated type of pad favoured by the makers of sporting rifles and some shot-guns is not suitable for target rifles, being too soft and resilient and permitting too much rearward movement of the rifle in recoil. In any case, recoil is not a problem that should bother any target shooter. If the rifle is held correctly (chapter 9), recoil should hardly be felt; the weight of modern target rifles appreciably reduces what little there is.

Fore-ends are generally of the wide (approx. 2½ inches) rounded variety. These give a comfortable hold for the average hand without the risk of the fingers extending over and touching the barrel—an occurrence which must be avoided because of its detrimental effect on accuracy.

One or two gunsmiths that specialise in catering for the target rifle marksman import Bishop walnut semi-finished stock blanks from America. These blanks, of selected straight grained American walnut of excellent quality, can be fitted to Mauser and P.'14/'17 rifles by a competent gunsmith. They have ample wood to provide individual fitting to suit the physical conformation of the shooter. After fitting for length, height of comb, fulness of grip etc., the stock is painstakingly re-surfaced and sealed with french polish. Chequering of pistol grip and fore-end is permitted and undoubtedly adds to the appearance and handling qualities of a rifle. Rifles fitted with hand-finished stocks are generally described as 'custom made', being specifically prepared for an individual purchaser. Considering their general excellence it is surprising that they cost little more than commercially made rifles.

Beech target stocks of English make can be obtained in a variety of styles for Mauser, P.'14/'17 and other rifles. They are less expensive and are usually described as 'economy' stocks.

They are, however, extremely good and can be individually fitted if required. They, too, are re-surfaced and french polished. The natural colour of the wood is very light and does not take stain too well. These stocks usually present a rather blonde appearance which is not unattractive.

Military style stocks can be produced by modifying the existing Service woodwork, cutting off an inch or two beyond the upper sling swivel and allowing the uncovered barrel to protrude from that point. A handguard is fitted and held in position by a retaining ring around the re-inforce and the middle band. The No. 4 rifle can be fitted with a Monte Carlo butt with cheek-piece etc. (see plates 12 to 15 for illustrations of various stock styles).

SIGHTING. All the aforementioned rifles are fitted with inter-changeable tunnel foresights, to which a variety of metal ring or blade elements can be fitted. Backsights are of the conventional match type with lateral and vertical adjustment in either half or quarter-minute increments. Target sights can be readily fitted to P.'14/'17 and No. 4 rifles without modification but Mauser and other rifles of foreign make are usually fitted with a simple adaptor plate or bracket to which the sight is fixed. In some cases modification to the sight base is necessary. Full details of sights, methods of fitting, zeroing etc. will be found in chapter 6 —'Sighting, Grouping and Zeroing'.

HANDSTOPS. For the first time under N.R.A. rules, handstops became a permitted refinement, with the introduction of the target rifle. Fitted to the underside of the fore-end, there are two types in general use on small bore rifles, which can be easily adapted for target rifles. Each comprises a metal handstop —usually of aluminium alloy—through which passes a screw incorporating the sling swivel. This either threads direct into a steel bar—drilled and tapped with a number of suitable holes— or engages in a square-headed nut which runs in a metal channel. In either case the steel bar, or the channel, is inletted into the underside of the fore-end and positioned to provide a number of conveniently placed settings to suit the firer. Handstops are usually used with single-point slings but can equally well be employed with two-point slings.

IN GENERAL. Obviously, a shooter is faced with a problem when making a choice from the wide selection of available target rifles. Some guidance is given in chapter 12 (Shooting Equipment) and the following generalisations are offered:

*1. The Mauser type of forward locking actions usually have 'negative compensation' and are therefore likely to be the best at short ranges, i.e. up to 600 yards.

*2. The rear-locking Lee-Enfield actions have pronounced 'positive compensation' and are therefore likely to be the best long range rifles, i.e. from 600 to 1,000 yards.

3. While all types of rifles should shoot better with good ammunition, some barrels seem to do better than others with indifferent ammunition.

4. Stock styles are a matter of personal preference, but in making a choice the emphasis should always be on comfort. Having once experienced the pleasure of shooting with a well fitted target rifle stock, few will wish to revert to the 'bare bones' of normal Service woodwork.

*There are exceptions to 1 and 2 above but the comments are based on a good deal of practical shooting and trials in the United Kingdom and Canada.

4

BEDDING AND REGULATING
TARGET RIFLES

For many years the bedding and regulating of .303 in. Lee-Enfield type Rifles for target shooting presented gunsmiths and armourers with a never ending and largely thankless task. There is no doubt that but for the devoted efforts of the few who were willing and able to undertake this frequently unprofitable work, particularly when the S.M.L.E. was the only rifle in general use, many devotees of competitive shooting may well have given it up in despair. The Lee-Enfield in its 'as issued' state was insufficiently accurate for target shooting and often caused much frustration and little pleasure to its users. However, these pioneers of the technique of bedding and regulating rifles eventually produced results of a relatively high order and thus played a large part in maintaining interest in full-bore target shooting in the United Kingdom and Commonwealth.

The manner in which a barrel vibrates when a round is fired, and the effect of the vibrations, has been described in chapter 2. It should therefore be appreciated that, for the best results to be obtained from a target rifle, the vibratory behaviour of the barrel must be consistent from shot to shot and from one shoot to the next.

Ideally, all bullets should leave the muzzle when it is at its neutral position—at the top or bottom of the vibratory movement. This would ensure that errors due to velocity variations would be reduced to a minimum, particularly at the shorter ranges. A few rifles appear to have this characteristic but the majority discharge the bullet at some point in the barrel's upward or downward stroke and are described as having positive or negative compensation respectively. To obtain the best results, perfect ammunition with little or no muzzle velocity variation is needed. With this, each bullet would leave the barrel at the same point in its vibratory movement and consequently would follow the same trajectory. As explained in chapter 6, ammunition particularly if mass produced, is subject to manufacturing tolerances which, even though kept to a minimum, inevitably produce individual variations.

There is little that can be done to make much material alteration to the overall barrel vibration pattern with the heavy target rifles now in vogue. With the more slender type of service barrel employed when all full-bore target shooting was done with the .303 in. cartridge, it was possible to control or damp the vibrations by applying tension or curvature to the barrel by the use of packing materials such as rubber, cork and certain plastics. As the .303 in. standard Service rifle is still in use in many places and likely to remain so until supplies of .303 in. ammunition are exhausted, a description of the most successful method of bedding and regulating this type of rifle may be useful. It should be remembered, however, that this is not a job for an amateur, many years of experience and training are necessary before first class results can be regularly achieved. The inexpert can do much damage to a rifle and entail considerable expense in replacement of damaged components.

CENTRE BEDDING THE No. 4 RIFLE. This method, one of three approved by the National Rifle Association soon after the second world war and in use ever since, has proved extremely satisfactory in achieving a highly uniform standard of accuracy. During the war it was initiated on sniper rifles in India and was afterwards submitted to extensive trials at Enfield. It is approved for weapons used by Schools Cadet Forces which represent a considerable proportion of those still using the .303 in. No. 4 Rifle.

The method consists of obtaining good bearing surfaces between the underside of the action body (receiver) and the fore-end wood, a firm fit and good bearing surfaces at the base of the fore-end and draws, and a good seating under the barrel reinforce (figure 14). Additionally, a bearing or seating is made for the barrel at a point five inches forward of the reinforce. This bearing should be approximately $1\frac{1}{2}$ ins. in length and the barrel should be clear of the woodwork from this point forward. Sufficient wood should be removed from the fore-end and front handguard at the muzzle end to ensure that no interference can take place (figures 14 and 15).

A stock fore-end absorbs a considerable amount of recoil each time the rifle is fired. This inevitably causes looseness in the fit of the woodwork. The relationship of fore-end to barrel becomes inconsistent, affecting the barrel vibrations and, consequently, the rifle's accuracy.

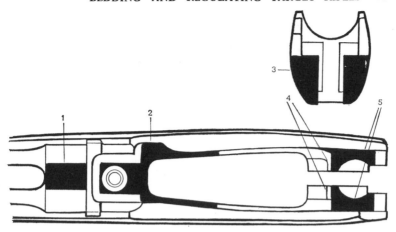

Fig. 14. Main body bearings—No. 4 rifle.

1 Reinforce.
2 Front action or body flats.
3 Base of fore-end.

4 Draws.
5 Rear action or body flats.

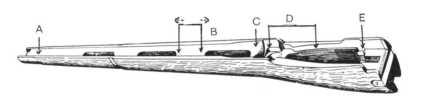

Fig. 15. No. 4 rifle (Service pattern) stock fore-end.

A Muzzle bearing.
B Centre bearing.
C Reinforce.

D Body.
E The draws.

To bring an 'as issued' Service rifle up to the standard required for target shooting, it is necessary to fit inserts of hard wood at those places which are subjected to recoil and where heavy pressure is applied—such as the draws and beneath the forward end of the trigger-guard (figure 14). One of the most suitable woods to use for this purpose is hornbeam—a white wood of considerable density and toughness which satisfactorily absorbs recoil. A metal plate may be fitted under the forward end of the trigger-guard. The accurate fitting and subsequent 'cutting on' of the wood blocks calls for considerable skill, and at the same time the base of the fore-end must be eased to give uniform and symmetrical bearings.

Good and well-fitting bearings are essential if the two surfaces

—generally metal and wood—are to remain in correct relationship. The process of obtaining good bearings is often a lengthy one, during which the woodwork may have to be removed and replaced many times before perfection is attained. To enable bearings to be inspected during construction, the metal surface is painted with blue marking paint or lamp-black—both mixed with oil—which are applied with a small brush.

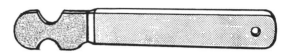

Fig. 16. A scraper used for perfecting bearings. Made from
an old table knife.

When the metal surface and fore-end are brought together in their correct relative position, high spots in the bearing will be clearly shown by the paint adhering to them. These high spots must then be eased down by careful scraping. A simple scraper can be made from an old table knife (figure 16). When a satisfactory bearing has been obtained it should be coated with a thin film of graphite and oil which, after a while will result in a smooth shiny appearance.

The amateur who does not consider his gunsmithing skill sufficient to make good new bearings by wood inserts can make a serviceable job by using fibre-glass or epoxy-resin putty. These materials are usually in two parts, one being the catalyst which, when mixed with the other component, starts the setting process.

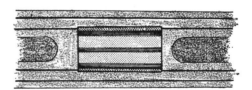

Fig. 17. Stocking-up No. 4 rifle. Barrel seating in
normal position in No. 4 rifle fore-end. Bearing
surfaces, approximately one-third of barrel circumference with central groove.

This results in extremely hard bearings, and there is very little shrinkage during the action of setting. The only serious disadvantage to bearings made in this manner is that once they have set they are not easily corrected, should any correction be necessary. Their removal frequently results in so much damage to the woodwork to which they are affixed that one is committed

Plate 16. Cold swaging machine for barrel manufacture, at the Enfield Royal Small Arms factory.

Plate 17 *(below)*. Conversion kit for No. 4 rifle showing four breeching washers of different thicknesses.

Plate 18 *(below)*. Barrel breeching rig with operator applying the torque wrench. In this instance, a barrel is being fitted to a No. 4 rifle action.

16

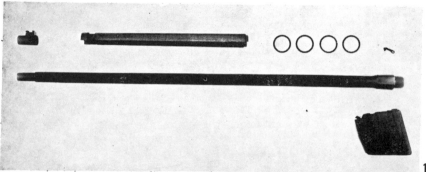

17

18

to the acceptance of bearings as made or to replacement of the complete fore-end.

The barrel seating (figure 17) is generally made between the lightening grooves in the fore-end, approximately five inches forward of the reinforce. This position is not abitrary however, and excellent results have been achieved when it has been positioned further forward, either in the second lightening groove, which must be filled up for this purpose, or in the vicinity of the middle band (figure 18). As a general rule the first method is quite satisfactory and it is the only one permitted in rifles that are Government property, i.e. those issued to Cadet units and similar organizations. This seating is best made with epoxy-resin putty, lined with fairly thick walnut or beech veneer

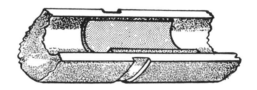

Fig. 18. Barrel seating in No. 4 rifle fore-end. In this instance it is shown at the middle band, but it is more usually positioned between the first and second lightening cuts.

which comes in contact with the barrel. The actual bearing surface extends for approximately one-third of the barrel's circumference, and a narrow groove made in the bottom to ensure that the barrel seats firmly and with no tendency to float about on high spots. The bearing should be finally coated with graphite and oil, and the barrel and action slightly 'sprung' between the back flat bearings and the barrel seating (figure 14) i.e. when the main trigger-guard screw is loosened, there should be a clearance of up to .005 in. between the front flat bearings of the action and the wood of the fore-end.

The basic fitting of the barrel and action to the fore-end should be carried out before the barrel seating is made, using the existing muzzle bearing as a guide to indicate that barrel and woodwork are correctly aligned. In addition, correct pressure at the muzzle end—about 4 to 5 lbs—is important. See figure 19 for method of testing weight of muzzle bearing. This is regulated by easing, or building up the reinforce bearing, thin walnut veneer being used for the latter process. The barrel seating, made as described above, should lift the barrel fractionally clear of the muzzle bearing. When set, the rifle can be finished off and re-

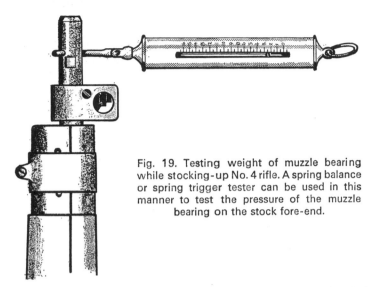

Fig. 19. Testing weight of muzzle bearing while stocking-up No. 4 rifle. A spring balance or spring trigger tester can be used in this manner to test the pressure of the muzzle bearing on the stock fore-end.

assembled, sufficient wood being removed from the inside of the fore-end and handguards to ensure that no interference with the barrel can occur. The two bands securing the handguards must be firmly secured and prevent sideways movement of the handguards which could result in their touching the barrel.

No. 4 RIFLE WITH HEAVY BARREL. Most of the bedding method described for the No. 4 Rifle is applicable when it is converted to 7.62 mm by fitting a heavy target style barrel. These barrels have a reinforce of similar shape to that of the .303 in. barrel so it is possible for similar bearing surfaces to be employed. The main difference is that the heavy 7.62 mm barrel should be 'fully floating' or free from contact with the woodwork from the reinforce forward. Experiments were carried out using a barrel seating five inches forward of the reinforce, but results obtained were indifferent and in some cases definitely bad until the bearing was removed.

Marks 1 and 2 of the No. 4 Rifle are suitable for adaption to take the 7.62 mm heavy target barrel. The Mark 2 type (figure 20), which has the trigger mechanism mounted on the action body, is recommended, being less liable to trigger troubles. However, if the Mark 1 type fore-end is properly fitted and bedded to eliminate all movement, the pull-off should remain constant for a reasonable length of time.

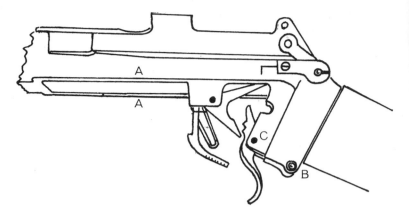

Fig. 20. No. 4 rifle body (Mark 2) and trigger mechanism.

A   Body walls each side of magazine opening.
B   Rear trigger-guard screw.
C   Trigger hung on body (Mark 2 body).

The fore-end is cut off approximately one inch forward of the middle band and the exposed lightening groove filled with a wood plug or suitable cement. A specially made long hand-guard is fitted. It is generally made oversize so that it can be taken down to suit the varying widths of rifle fore-end. When fitted, the barrel must be well clear of the woodwork and completely exposed for a distance of approximately 14-ins. back from the muzzle.

The only drawback from a mechanical viewpoint of the No. 4 Rifle is that there are many wartime rifles still in use and the material from which these were made was sometimes inferior to that used in more normal circumstances. Such material was often difficult to harden and in consequence some of these wartime No. 4's have soft bolt lugs. These are generally discovered when the rifle is submitted for Nitro Proof but the tendency is there, and a periodic inspection of bolt-lugs and check on cartridge headspace is advisable.

THE BEDDING OF MAUSER TYPE RIFLES. The basic principles of bedding and adjusting Mauser type rifles are applicable to most rifles with one-piece stocks, i.e. as distinct from the Lee-Enfield rifles with separate butt and fore-end sections. In most Mauser and similar actions the receiver portion is held in position by two screws passing through the trigger-guard into threaded holes in the underside of the action body. These screws, known as the front and rear trigger-guard screws, are generally about ¼ in. in diameter. Most actions of this type have a transverse recoil shoulder on the underside of the body, and frequently the front trigger-guard screw is threaded into this shoulder (see figure 11, Chapter 3 which shows a Mauser action in detail). The recoil shoulder bears against a corresponding shoulder or seating in the woodwork.

At one time rifles of this type were bedded directly into the woodwork of the stock, and looseness or ill-fitting bearings were made up with inserts of veneer or even metal shims. Eventually, the bearings would give way and sometimes break through altogether, causing the rear tang to split the butt. Most military Mauser stocks have a metal bolt set transversely at the recoil shoulder to minimise this possibility. Target rifle stocks are not usually so fitted.

Now that epoxy resins and fibre-glass cements are readily available and easily applied, their use for bedding target rifles has become universally accepted, and there is no doubt that certain of these compounds are eminently suitable and effective. They have the added advantage that they do not shrink to any great extent.

Bearing surfaces for the action body are obtained by seating in a suitable compound on either side of the front guard screw; sufficient wood being removed to provide for an adequate thickness of the compound. It is customary to remove sufficient wood to allow at least ⅜ inch behind the recoil shoulder as this is the point at which the maximum stress occurs. A similar bearing is made around the rear trigger-guard screw, the wood usually being removed by a milling cutter to make a neat recess (plate 22). The cement forming the front and rear bearings is put in at the same time and the screws tightened evenly and the action body drawn down to its correct position. The barrel should lie centrally and at the correct height in the barrel groove. It must be remembered that once the bearings are made they cannot be altered. If they are incorrect, the whole lot must be cut out, with probable damage to the rifle stock. It must also be remembered that metal surfaces, including screws, must be liberally coated with oil or similar freeing agent to ensure that the cement does not adhere to the metalwork. If this precaution is not taken, the barrel, action and woodwork become locked solidly together and cannot be separated except by the complete destruction of the stock.

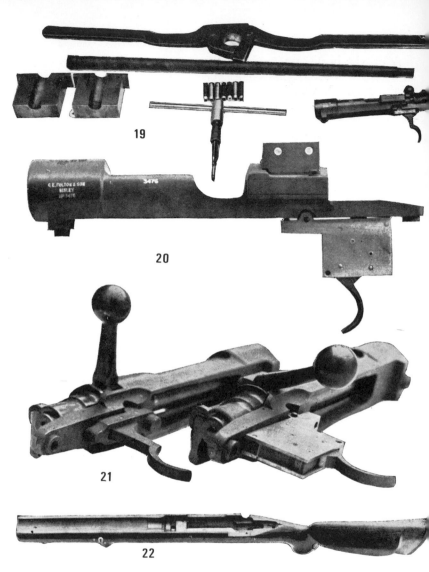

Plate 19. *Top* Barrel wrench.
Centre 7.62 mm Kongsberg rifle barrel.
Bottom (*left to right*) Clams for re-barrelling vice. Chambering reamer and depth gauges. Mauser '98 action body.

Plate 20. Mauser action body, fitted with Schultz & Larsen match trigger and bracket to accommodate aperture backsight.

Plate 21. Modification to Mauser bolt handle. The right is ɑ modified handle and the action body is fitted with a match trigger. Left is a handle in its original state and the trigger is the normal service pattern.

Plate 22. A target rifle one-piece stock, as fitted to a Mauser action. The principal bearings are in the vicinity of the two action screws.

After the body bearings have set, recesses can be cut under both ends of the trigger-guard, and similar hard bearings made to absorb the tightening of the guard screws. If desired, the stud or boss surrounding the front screw on Mauser rifles can be reduced by half its length. It serves no useful purpose and could be a positive disadvantage if it should result in a metal to metal contact between the trigger-guard and the underside of the action body. It is important that the action body itself bears evenly and symmetrically on its seating and that it is under no stress or torsion when the screws are tightened.

If desired the barrel may be supported on bedding compound for up to one inch at the breech end, but must be completely clear of the woodwork from that point forward. Clearance can be checked by passing a card between barrel and woodwork.

TRIGGERS AND TRIGGER PRESSURES. Most modern military rifles, irrespective of country of origin, incorporate a two-stage or double pressure system in their trigger pulls, primarily designed as a safety measure. Earlier rifles such as the Snider, Martini-Henry and early Marks of Lee-Enfield had one-stage pulls.

When only standard Service rifles were permitted under N.R.A. rules it was often difficult to obtain trigger pressures satisfying target shooting requirements with the equipment available. Since the adoption of the new rules governing target rifle shooting, however, modern adjustable or 'Match' triggers have been permitted and undoubtedly represent a considerable improvement over the standard mechanism.

For many years the minimum permissible pull-off weight was 5-lbs., measured with the rifle held at an angle of 25 degrees to the vertical (plate 23). Inevitably, this angle, usually being dependent on personal assessment, was apt to vary when the trigger was tested. Under present Target Rifle rules, rifles are held vertically and the minimum weight a trigger must lift is 1.5 kg (approximately 3 lb. 5½ oz.) (plate 24).

SERVICE RIFLE TRIGGERS AND THEIR ADJUSTMENT. Two-stage trigger mechanisms all operate on the same basic principle. The cocking-piece, with striker and spring, is held in the cocked position by the sear. The sear is released by the trigger pivoting on its axis pin and bringing two raised ribs into operation (figure 21). The amount of movement required to rotate the trigger from the first to the second rib determines the length of

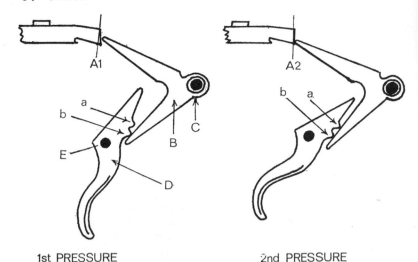

1st PRESSURE   2nd PRESSURE

Fig. 21. No. 4 rifle trigger mechanism and pull-off. Relative positions of trigger, sear and bent. To reduce the weight of the pull-off, increase the angle made by the face of the bent (A1) with the vertical. To increase the weight, reduce the angle (A2). Use an oilstone for the purpose.

A   Face of bent.   E   Trigger axis.
B   Sear.   (a)   Upper rib.
C   Sear axis.   (b)   Lower rib.
D   Trigger.

the first trigger pressure. If this is too great the sear will be moved clear of the bent before the second rib can bear on the sear (figure 21). This will eliminate the second pressure; accurate shooting with a rifle in this state is practically impossible. Additionally, the pull-off will be too light to lift the minimum weight. If the movement between the rib is insufficient, the sear will not be brought right to the edge of the bent, and when the second pressure is taken there will be a further movement known as 'drag' before the striker is released. This, too, will have a detrimental effect on the final aim.

The actual weight of trigger pressure is determined by the angle of the bent face and the weight of sear spring (figure 20). Normally, adjustment is made on the bent face by means of an India oilstone, operating the stone at right-angles to the direction of sear movement and finishing off by polishing upwards and downwards, i.e. in the direction in which the sear operates (see figure 21 for adjustment procedure). No sharp edge should be

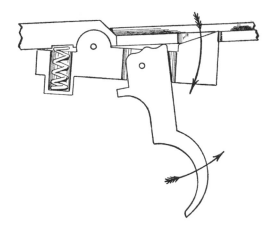

Fig. 22. Normal trigger mechanism of Mauser action.

left at the corner of the bent face, and it is advisable to smooth the engaging surface of the sear. Lubrication of the bent is effected by means of graphite or pencil lead. If the pull-off weight cannot be satisfactorily reduced by the foregoing method, a further small adjustment can be made by reducing the weight of the sear spring. If this is a coil spring, as in Mauser actions (figure 22), a small amount can be removed and the end ground square. If a flat V-spring, as in Lee-Enfield rifles, the long arm can be reduced in thickness by careful grinding. It must be remembered that in Lee-Enfield rifles the magazine catch exerts pressure on the sear spring, and therefore the magazine must always be assembled when testing. Great care must be exercised when reducing the sear spring weight of either type of rifle. If excessive, the sear will not recover its position on the bent face when pressure, without firing, is applied to the trigger. This can be most embarrassing to a firer on aim, especially in a coached shoot when wind changes are frequently called.

Adjustment of a trigger embodies the correction of pull-off weight and the removal of 'drag'. As the two are interdependent they must, to some extent, be done together. Usually, the bent receives attention first and, when this is smooth and gives approximately the correct weight of pull-off, any necessary adjustments are made to the ribs to ensure a crisp trigger release. By placing the fore-finger around the trigger until the tip comes in contact with the trigger-guard and applying a slow and careful squeeze with the whole finger, any 'drag' on the second pressure will become apparent. A very small safety margin is desirable and can be assessed in this manner.

If there is too much 'drag' when the first pressure is applied, the sear must be made to travel slightly further down the bent face. This is achieved by reducing the height of the rib furthest from the trigger axis pin. If the metal is soft, this can be done with a sharp file. If hard, by judicious grinding with a fine emery wheel. Removal of a very small amount will be sufficient, and the profile of the rib must be retained. To rectify a pull-off that 'goes right through', i.e. has no second pressure, the other rib must be reduced. This one, being nearer the trigger axis, is more sensitive than its counterpart. Having satisfactorily adjusted the ribs, a final polish should now be applied to the bent face with an oilstone. This will ensure a smooth first pressure.

MATCH TRIGGERS. Most Mauser type rifles, including the P.'14, can be fitted with a match trigger, and this excellent accessory is strongly recommended. A match trigger consists of a housing containing a trigger and sear with various adjusting screws and springs, and it is attached to the underside of the action body in place of the standard trigger (figure 23 and plate 20, chapter 3).

When the action is cocked, the cocking-piece, striker etc., are held in the normal cocked position by the sear. When the trigger—whether one or two stage, depending on the type of mechanism—is pressed, the sear is released or tripped and falls forward under the weight of the striker spring, allowing the striker to travel forward and fire the cartridge. The essence of the match trigger is that it comprises precision made hardened components which are controlled by light springs. The trigger is adjustable for weight and 'drag' and, in some cases, what the Americans call 'backlash', i.e. over-travel after sear release.

Some triggers have their adjusting screws fitted with lock nuts to ensure tightness in use. Others do not, in which case it is advisable for the screw controlling the trigger weight to be secured by some means to prevent it from coming unscrewed and causing the trigger to lose weight unobserved by the firer. A small application of Locktite (a commercial product for locking screws) is effective.

A word of warning is necessary at this stage. Certain types of match triggers when fitted to P.'14 and M.'17 rifles have too much metal on the engaging face of the sear, with the result that

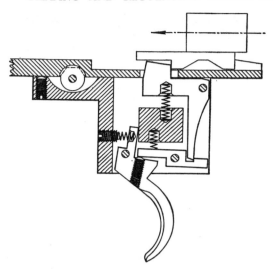

Fig. 23. The mechanism of a match trigger for Mauser M.98
type actions.

if the safety-catch is applied and the trigger pressed, the sear is carried forward a small amount and is not able to recover to the cocked position. When the safety-catch is pushed forward the striker mechanism is released and if a cartridge is in the chamber, will fire it. The cure is simple and consists of the removal of metal from either the sear or bent face until the safety-catch can be applied and the trigger pressed with impunity.

TRIGGER TESTING. It is essential that a marksman should know how to test his own trigger so that he can be certain that it is unlikely to fail if tested on the range. The penalty for failure in competitive shooting is disallowance of the score. As triggers are normally tested at prize meetings after a good shoot—usually a 'highest possible' score—failure to pass the test can completely ruin a meeting for the unfortunate competitor.

The best type of trigger tester is the deadweight variety, and this is applied to the trigger with the rifle held in the vertical position (plate 24). The steadiest method is with the weight on a level floor and the rifle held with both hands, the forearms being rested on the knees. By this method a very gradual lifting motion

Plate 23. The old method of trigger testing. In this illustration, competitors are having their triggers tested before shooting in the final stage of the Queen's Prize.

Plate 24. The present method of testing the weight of a target rifle trigger. In competitive shooting at Bisley this is usually done on a table on the firing-point.

Plate 25. 7.62 mm 'F.N.' self-loading rifle.

25

can be achieved and the weight of the pull-off accurately assessed.

To safeguard against a light pull-off and the risk entailed, it is recommended that the pull-off weight should be four to six ounces more than the minimum permitted.

5

THE CARTRIDGE

The 7.62 mm NATO round is now used in British target shooting, having superseded the .303 in. cartridge which was in use in the United Kingdom and Commonwealth countries for many years. Both are classified as 'Small Arm Cartridges'—a classification that embraces all calibres for use in rifles, machine-guns, sub-machine-guns, pistols and revolvers up to .5 in.

The 7.62 mm was originally the T.65 cartridge designed in the United States shortly after the Second World War. After many comparative trials it was selected by the North Atlantic Treaty Organization. It was adopted by the British, Australian, Canadian, New Zealand and South African armed forces for use with self-loading rifles. The .303 in. was the last of a long line of rimmed cartridges whereas the 7.62 mm is rimless. This makes it more suitable for use in automatic arms due to its ease of feeding from belts, magazines etc. Both cartridges are shown at figure 24.

The 7.62 mm cartridge gives satisfactory ballistics if of high quality manufacture. Though smaller and lighter than the .303 in., it gives improved accuracy at the longer range due to its boat-tailed (streamlined) bullet, less barrel erosion, and longer barrel accuracy life. Its storage life is also longer due to the use of a non-mercuric anti-corrosive cap composition. It has a higher muzzle velocity and flatter trajectory (figure 25) and is slightly less affected by wind, particularly at short ranges. In Match Rifle shooting a heavier bullet is used for its greater stability at extreme ranges.

The principal components of a small arm cartridge are the case, percussion cap, propellant charge and bullet.

THE CASE. The cartridge case is usually made of brass because it is strong, non-rusting, well suited to methods of manufacture and of suitable weight. Cartridge brass must be of high quality and should contain about 70% of copper and 30% of zinc, with

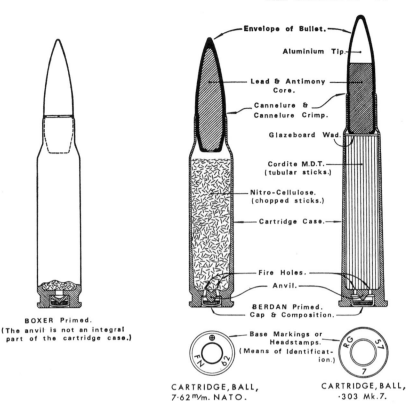

BOXER Primed.
(The anvil is not an integral
part of the cartridge case.)

Envelope of Bullet.
Aluminium Tip.
Lead & Antimony Core.
Cannelure & Cannelure Crimp.
Glazeboard Wad.
Cordite M.D.T. (tubular sticks.)
Nitro-Cellulose. (chopped sticks.)
Cartridge Case.
Fire Holes.
Anvil.
BERDAN Primed. Cap & Composition.
Base Markings or Headstamps. (Means of Identification.)

CARTRIDGE, BALL,
7·62 m/m. NATO.

CARTRIDGE, BALL,
·303 Mk.7.

Fig. 24. Comparison of cartridges.

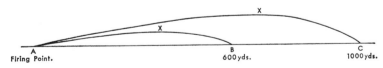

A
Firing Point.

B
600 yds.

C
1000 yds.

Fig. 25. Bullet speeds and trajectories. Based on a nominal muzzle velocity of
2,750 f.p.s., a 145 grain 7.62 mm NATO bullet travels from A to B in approximately 0.87 secs. with maximum trajectory height X of 3.1 ft. and from A to C
in approximately 1.81 secs. with maximum trajectory height X of 11.2 ft.

very small traces of other impurities. This composition produces
an alloy that will withstand the severe strains imposed on a
cartridge case. Suitable steels have also been used in case
manufacture.

The case is made slightly cone-shaped to ease withdrawal
from the rifle chamber after the cartridge has been fired, and it

is bottle-necked to avoid undue length yet still provide adequate capacity for the propellant charge. The neck of the case is usually varnished internally to improve waterproofing. This, however, is something of a disadvantage from an accuracy viewpoint—as is heavy crimping or indenting—due to its effect on the pressure required to drive the bullet out of the case. The base of the case is grooved to facilitate extraction.

CAP CHAMBER. The percussion cap chamber is sited at the base of the case, access from it to the body of the case which contains the propellant charge being given by one or two fire holes (figure 24). The cap composition is detonated by being compressed between the striker and a raised nipple called the anvil. In the majority of British made cartridges the anvil is an integral part of the cap chamber, the two fire holes being on either side of it. In such cases, the Berdan type of cap (figure 24) is used.

Certain American and Continental cartridges use the Boxer type cap, which has its anvil as a separate component built into the cap. In this case, the cap chamber is a simple depression in the base of the cartridge with a single, central fire hole (figure 24).

PERCUSSION CAP (PRIMER). The percussion cap is a small circular cup made of copper or brass. The material from which it is made is important. It must be sufficiently ductile to indent but not perforate when struck by the firing-pin and, after firing, to expand into the cap chamber and so form an efficient gas seal. It must also be stiff enough to resist ignition by accidental strike. In most British Service cartridges the cap is pressed into the cap chamber and secured by 'ringing', the metal of the cap chamber being pressed over the edge of the cap. Another method, much favoured in other countries, is known as 'punch stabbing', in which the cap is secured by three or four indentations at equal intervals around its edge. The cap must be a close fit to prevent escape of gas, and it must be flush with, or slightly below, the base of the cartridge case. Gas escaping around the cap will cause corrosion and erosion of the face of the bolt or breech-block in the form of a ring around the striker hole and may cause the cap to be loosened or even ejected from the cap chamber. If a pierced cap should result from an over-long or badly shaped striker point, brittle cap metal, or excessive pressure in the cap chamber, it may cause the striker and cocking-piece to be blown back, and forced into the 'half-cock' position on rifles which have this feature. This endangers the firer's eye from flying particles and almost certain breakage of spectacles, if worn. Lee-Enfield rifles have gas escape holes in the left side of the body (receiver) to minimise danger from burst caps or burst cases.

CAP COMPOSITION. Cap composition ingredients are very sensitive to shock or friction and are ignited by such means. Sub-quality materials or irregularities in composition result in uneven ignition, hangfires and misfires. Hangfires—the term applied to abnormal periods of time elapsing between the striking of the cap and the ignition of the propellant charge—can have a most detrimental effect on accuracy. The cap composition is fired by the blow of the striker on the cap and ignites the propellant charge via the fire holes. Regular ignition is essential for accuracy.

PROPELLANT CHARGE. Upon ignition, the propellant charge generates the gas pressure which imparts the driving force on the bullet and provides its velocity. To do this, the charge must burn—not detonate—and do so relatively slowly in order to maintain steady and progressive pressure on the base of the bullet.

The combustion rate of modern propellant is so controlled that the necessary gas pressure to provide the required bullet velocity is developed relatively quickly and the entire charge consumed before the bullet leaves the barrel. It is interesting to note that these explosives contain their own 'built in' oxygen supply and can therefore function in a completely sealed container, such as a cartridge case, without having to draw their oxygen from the air as do most other combustible materials.

The propellant in the British Service 7.62 mm cartridge is nitro-cellulose in the form of powder or chopped tube and is known as Nobel's Rifle Neonite and is a single base propellant. There are Neonites, notably NNN (Nobel's Nitro Neonite) which are double based. Cellulose, which is derived from certain types of plant and tree wood pulp or cotton (most frequently used), is subjected to a process of nitration by immersion in a mixture of nitric and sulphuric acids. Subsequently, after removal of the acids, it is treated with ether, diphenylamine and graphite and the gelatinised nitro-cellulose mixture is extruded into cords of the required size and chopped into short lengths. The grains of powder so produced are finally treated with dinitroluene to reduce the rate of burning during the early stages. This is described as a 'single base' propellant. There is no wad between the propellant and the bullet.

Propellants consisting of a mixture of nitro-cellulose and nitro-glycerine are also used and are known as 'double base' proprellants. Cordite—so called on account of its cord-like form—is an example, and was used in the British .303 in. cartridge for many years. Double base propellants are hotter burning than single base and also tend to develop maximum pressure more rapidly. Consequently they cause greater wear and tear on the barrel-lead due to erosion and intense localised pressure. In an attempt to minimise this, a glazeboard wad is used with cordite and is placed between the propellant charge and the base of the bullet to act as a gas check during the early critical period. Double base propellants give great initial punch causing the bullet, even in barrels with worn leads, to engage the rifling with maximum efficiency, so sealing the bore against escape of gas past the bullet. This expansion of the base of the bullet is known as 'set up'. It applies only to flat-based bullets.

THE BULLET. The bullet used in the 7.62 mm cartridge consists of a lead core encased in an envelope of gilding metal. Lead provides the required weight in proportion to size. Pure lead would be too soft to withstand the high velocity and rapid rotation of the modern bullet and it is therefore hardened with antimony. The bullet envelope must be sufficiently soft to engage the rifling but strong enough to withstand the stresses imposed upon it, both inside the barrel and in flight. The .303 in. bullet had an aluminium tip incorporated to position the centre of gravity towards the base of the bullet and so improve stability (figure 24)

The modern bullet is cylindro-ogival in shape and ideally should be fractionally larger than the bore of the weapon to ensure perfect obturation. Most bullets are now made with streamlined (boat-tailed) bases, the object being to minimise the drag or turbulence that normally develops behind a flat-based bullet. By reducing turbulence, the bullet flies more truly, maintains its velocity and trajectory, evolves less yaw (chapter 2) and in consequence considerably greater range is obtained. The base of the bullet is uncovered, the lead core being exposed to the propellant charge at this point.

The weight of the Nato Service bullet is 144 grains and this is the type generally used in Target Rifle shooting. Heavier bullets up to 180 grains are used for Match Rifle shooting where stability and the maintenance of velocity over extra long distances are required. The American National Match competition bullet is 173 grains; the same weight as the .303 in. Mark 7 bullet.

MARKING. The base of British made cartridge cases bear the following marking:
(a) The manufacturer's initials or recognised trade mark.
(b) The last two figures of the year of manufacture.
(c) The 'Mark', as applicable (figure 24).

The annulus of the cap is varnished with a coloured lacquer to identify the nature of the cartridge and also to assist waterproofing. The Target Rifle marksman need concern himself only with the ball cartridge; no others should be used. The annulus of the British Service ball round is coloured purple. Other countries have their own colour schemes which do not necessarily conform to the British.

STANDARD OF ACCURACY AND MANUFACTURE. British Service cartridges are manufactured to a Government specification and subjected to rigorous inspection and proof tests. Accuracy testing is normally carried out at a distance of 500 yards, and acceptance or rejection is based on the average results calculated from not less than four 20-round groups, known as the mean 'Figure of Merit'. The barrels used for accuracy testing are kept to a rigid standard, especially in regard to barrel bore and chamber dimensions, cartridge headspace and striker protrusion. They are breeched into an action, and the assembly bedded into a metal stock. This is held in a mechanical rest.

In determining the figure of merit of a group, the distance of each shot from the m.p.i. (centre of group) is carefully measured. The deviations are added together and the sum divided by the number of shots fired. Under this system the wider shots are cancelled out by those closer to the centre of the group. A batch, or lot, of ammunition varying in size from 100,000 to 200,000 rounds is accepted as having passed the Service accuracy test if the average figure of merit does not exceed 8 inches. Allowances are made in cases where the dispersion of a group has obviously been adversely affected by wind, i.e. blown shots. Most of the ammunition gives a much smaller figure of merit than the acceptance standard and the average of the Service 7.62 mm round is considered to be under 5.5 ins.

From the foregoing it will be seen that the figure of merit of any particular batch of ammunition is no guarantee that all the cartridges in the batch will group to that figure. Whilst many of the rounds will be well inside the limit, some—a very small percentage, perhaps—will not. Understanding of this point should give comfort to marksmen who otherwise might blame themselves, or their rifle, or the wind, when unexpectedly wide shots appear on their targets. Conversely, marksmen should not always assume that poor ammunition is responsible for low scores. Generally speaking, the 7.62 mm round used in target shooting gives a high standard of accuracy.

In the mass manufacture of, say, a million bullets, it is quite certain that not all will be of exactly the same weight and dimensions. If the centre of gravity is not precisely on the axis of the bullet—due to an envelope of uneven thickness or similar cause—that bullet will not spin truly, and when it leaves the barrel it will commence its flight on the line on which its centre of gravity is travelling. Despite the utmost care in manufacture, uneven bullet envelopes are not uncommon and are extremely difficult to detect.

The bullet envelope, and the cartridge case, is made by punching a disc out of metal strip which is then pressed into the form of a shallow cup. By a series of pressing operations, these cups are drawn out into thin tubes from which the finished product emerges. Within permissible limits, there are invariably slight variations in length, diameter, and wall thickness.

In the same way, variation in size, the application of stabiliser, and other small manufacturing defects can occur in connection with the propellant. These can affect the pressure and velocity to an extent which, though still within manufacturing tolerances, are detrimental to the high standards of accuracy demanded for target shooting.

Even the cap performance can vary (due to excessive varnish applied in the waterproofing process) and poor ignition, causing fluctuating velocities, can result.

These are just a few of the variables which can occur in the manufacture of small arms ammunition. Frequently, such variations cancel each other out. But on the rare occasions when they are all in the same direction, the unlucky marksman will almost certainly get an unaccountably wide shot.

PRECAUTIONARY MEASURES. Success in marksmanship is largely dependent on attention to detail, and this applies as much to the cartridge as to every other factor which has any bearing on accurate shooting. It is virtually impossible to pick out the good rounds from those which may be slightly inferior as there are no visual means of determining what is inside the cartridge case. There are, however, certain precautions which help towards ensuring the best possibile regularity from ammunition. They are as follows:

1. Examine the base markings of every cartridge, and ensure that all the ammunition used in a shoot is of the same make·and the same year of manufacture.

2. If ammunition is drawn in bulk, as is customary at a Bisley National Meeting, it will probably be issued in cardboard boxes. Each box will be marked with the manufactuer's initials and 'date of work' of the batch of ammunition from which the box has been filled, e.g., R.G. 27-3-70, denoting that the cartridges in the box were made at Radway Green Royal Ordance Factory and that the batch was accepted by the Inspector of Small Arms Ammunition on the 27th March, 1970.

3. It is important to ensure that all cartridges are reasonably clean and the cases free from oil, dust, or corrosion. The cases of cartridges which have been stored for several years sometimes show signs of corrosion.

4. If a misfire occurs, the cartridge should be left in the chamber for a few seconds before the bolt is opened. For although it is rare, there is always the possibility of a 'hangfire'. If the cap appears to have been lightly struck, the misfire will probably be due to insufficient striker protrusion or a weak mainspring. This is a job for the gun-smith or armourer. If the cap has been properly struck, the misfire is probably due to the cartridge and the round should be changed for another. Misfires of this nature are more likely to occur with old ammunition.

5. Cartridges should not be exposed to hot sunshine, neither should they be allowed to remain in a hot rifle chamber longer than is necessary. Propellant charges are influenced by temperature. If heated, they turn into gas more quickly, producing higher pressures. In hot weather, therefore, the time factor between loading and firing should be as short as possible. If, for some reason, there is a time-lag in aiming and firing, the cartridge should be ejected and replaced by another.

HAND LOADING. The practice of re-loading fired cartridge cases has long been in operation in the United States, and within recent years has attracted considerable attention in the United Kingdom, particularly among pistol shooters who use considerable quantities of ammunition and are less restricted by competition rules.

It is normal practice for ammunition only 'as issued' to be used in Target Rifle competitive shooting. This is reasonable as it ensures, as far as possible, all competitors shooting on equal terms. Hand loaded rifle cartridges are not normally permitted. When not shooting under competition rules, a shooter may use any make he pleases and there are a few competitions, principally confined to the Match Rifle, in which any ammunition may be used.

Hand loading is a complex subject and there are handbooks that deal exclusively with its various aspects. It is not our intention to go into the subject in detail, but merely to offer a few observations.

EQUIPMENT. It is poor economy to invest in a cheap or inefficient re-loading press, simply because of its low cost. For dealing with rifle cartridges, a strong press that can be used comfortably for long periods without exhausting the operator is required. If large quantities are to be re-loaded for a club or similar organization, a turret press is a good investment, or even better a small 'production line' of single presses each performing a different operation. A powder measure in the form of a 'hopper' or container with a micrometer device for the accurate measurement of charge weights can be introduced into the 'production line'.

Powder scales are an essential item of equipment and can be used to weigh each individual charge or for check-weighing powder charges measured by volume. The better scales have a damper of oil which accelerates the steadying of the scale beam thus speeding up the weighing process. The scale pan is shaped to facilitate pouring the powder into the cartridge case.

De-capping devices are avilable for the Berdan type of primer (figure 24) which is rather difficult to remove. The simplest is a pronged tool which fits the two fire-holes and pushes out the cap. Another type, used externally, pierces the cap and levers it out. Boxer primers are easily removed through the single fire-hole by a de-capping pin usually incorporated with one of the re-sizing dies mounted in the re-loading press.

Lead bullets can be cast in a variety of shapes and sizes, suitable mould blocks being available for the purpose. Another method, known as bullet swaging, consists of pressing short lengths of lead wire of appropriate thickness into suitably shaped and sized copper jackets. A special bullet swaging press is required for this, and the resultant bullet is jacketed for approximately half its length and has a projecting lead nose or point. Normally, for accurate target shooting, factory made fully jacketed bullets of high quality are used.

RE-LOADING COMPONENTS. Cartridge cases can be purchased already capped, or can be salvaged from fired cartridges. It is often easier and more economical to buy good quality commercially loaded cartridges and save the cases after firing. Normally they are good for about twenty re-loads and, as they become fatigued, can be replaced by new cases. An early decision should be made whether to use Berdan or Boxer primed cases. The former primers are cheaper but harder to remove and it may be considered that the ease of removal of the Boxer type outweighs their relatively high cost. The two types are not interchangeable.

For a high degree of accuracy, there is no room for economy in bullets.The best target bullets are imported and can be had in a variety of different weights. The lighter ones of around 150 grains being suitable for ranges up to 600 yards, and heavier bullets up to 180 grains for the long ranges up to 1,200 yards. Cast lead bullets are not really suitable for target shooting and are not recommended.

British made re-loading powder is available in four varieties for rifle cartridges and three for pistol and revolver cartridges. They are of high quality and are of the nitro-cellulose single base type. The intending re-loader is advised to obtain the small booklet published by the manufacturers of these powders and carefully study the recommended loads before commencing operations. Re-loading must be properly done and care must be exercised at all times. The foregoing observations apply also to American powders when they are available. There are some excellent American handbooks on the subject of re-loading and bullet casting.

6

SIGHTING, ZEROING AND GROUPING

THEORY OF SIGHTING. The sighting system enables the rifle to be aimed at the target, the sights being placed conveniently to the firer's eye when the rifle is held in the firing position.

Theoretically, there are two imaginary lines from a rifle that is directed at a target. These are the line of sight and the arc of trajectory. Correctly used, the sighting system ensures the intersection of the two lines at the intended point of impact of the bullet (figure 26 and figure 4, chapter 2).

Fig. 26.

A   Backsight.
B   Foresight.
A—B   Sight radius.
A—X   Line of sight.
C   Point of departure of bullet.
D   Where lines of sight and trajectory intersect (centre of target).
Because the line of sight is higher than the line of projection, the trajectory is lower than the line of sight for a short distance. D is therefore the second intersection of the lines of sight and trajectory.

As a marksman does not necessarily aim directly at his objective, the sights must be constructed to permit the line of sight to be directed at any point in the target area at any range used in target shooting. The reason for this is explained in chapter eleven. The sights must therefore embody the means for making accurate adjustments in order that the muzzle of the rifle can:

  (a) be elevated to the requisite angle to allow for the fall of the bullet.
  (b) be directed to either side of the trajectory to correct lateral errors on the target.

Foresights on modern target rifles are fixed; all necessary

means of adjustment being embodied in the backsight. Raising the backsight eyepiece has the effect of depressing the breech end of the barrel, giving the muzzle the required elevation, and allowing the line of sight to remain constant.

Because the muzzle is elevated, the line of sight is above the trajectory at the commencement of a bullet's flight and there will be an early point of intersection (figure 26 and figure 4, chapter 2). The more the muzzle is elevated, the closer it will be to the point of intersection.

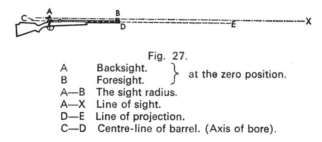

Fig. 27.

A	Backsight.	} at the zero position.
B	Foresight.	
A—B	The sight radius.	
A—X	Line of sight.	
D—E	Line of projection.	
C—D	Centre-line of barrel. (Axis of bore).	

THE SIGHTING SCALE. The sighting scale is a graduated measurement of the amount the backsight must be raised to give the barrel the correct elevation for the required range. The scale is based on the 'zero' position of the sights. This is when the line of sight and the line of projection are parallel (figure 27). On most Target Rifles the 'zero' position of the line of sight is between 1 and 1½ ins. above the line of projection. The graduations—in yards—are determined by the bullet's trajectory and are as correct as possible for the combination of rifle and cartridge for which they are designed. Thus, a sighting scale may not be correct for any other rifle and/or cartridge.

BACKSIGHTS. Aperture backsights are in general use in target shooting, embodying an eyepiece containing a small circular hole for aiming. The sights are made to a high standard of precision and constructed to allow vertical and horizontal movement of the eyepiece. The vertical movement is obtained by moving the sight arm (with eyepiece) in the main block which is rigidly attached to the rifle. In most sights this arm can be entirely removed by means of a quick release mechanism, but is capable of fine adjustment to give the desired elevation settings. Laterally, the eyepiece is moved along the sight arm.

Adjustments in both planes are made by the use of knurled knobs (figure 28). A clicking device, comprising spring-loaded

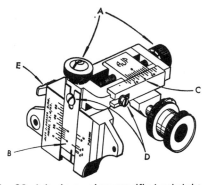

Fig. 28. A 'twin zero' target rifle backsight.
A   Knurled knobs for making sight adjustments.
B   Vertical (range/elevation) scale plate.
C   Lateral (windage) scale plate.
D   Set screws.
E   Slide release.

small steel balls which engage in grooves cut in the underside of the knobs, is incorporated to indicate the amount of movement effected. The eyepiece is adjustable for size of aperture (figure 29). The principle of this type of sight—originally known as an orthoptic sight—is similar to that of stopping down a camera lens to obtain depth of focus. And as a camera iris is adjusted to meet the prevailing light conditions, variable aperture eyepieces are used by marksmen to give the best possible definition.

KNURLED
EDGE

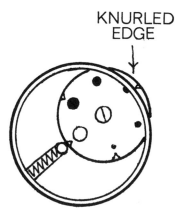

Fig. 29. Principle of 6-hole eyepiece. The desired aperture is obtained by turning the knurled eye-piece. When changing apertures, great care should always be taken to ensure that the moving plate has firmly clicked into position. Failing to do this has lost many marksmen valuable points.

SIGHT SCALES AND SIGHT PLATES. Sight readings are referred to in minutes of angle, or more generally as 'minutes'. A true minute of angle subtends 1.047 ins. at 100 yards. The first aperture backsights used in British target shooting were designed for the Long Lee-Enfield Rifle. This had a sight radius of about 35 ins. and the sight graduations were designed to approximate a true minute of angle. With the advent of the Short Lee-Enfield Rifle, and later the No. 4 Rifle, which had shorter sight radii, the effect of the sight minute became progressively coarser. The introduction of the Target Rifle with its longer barrel has rectified this to some extent, and the effect of an 'aperture sight minute' is sufficiently close to one inch per hundred yards for all practical purposes.

The adjusting knobs are designed to give half-minute or quarter-minute clicks. The majority of older Target Rifle marksmen have learned to shoot with the former, and in normal to strong winds, and with the target dimensions as they have been for many years, half-minute clicks have been found satisfactory. Modern Target Rifles and high quality 7.62 mm cartridges have however, caused target scoring dimensions to be reduced and in these circumstances half-minute clicks may be found too coarse. A finer adjustment is considered more necessary at short ranges than at long.

All modern sights have adjustable scale plates held in position by small screws, and slotted so that they can be moved as desired when 'zeroing'. The elevation scale besides being graduated in minutes of angle is inscribed with the ranges in yards, in increments of 100 yards. The lateral or wind scale is inscribed in minutes of angle on either side of a central zero mark (figures 28 and 30).

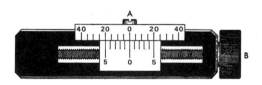

Fig. 30 Lateral (windage arm)

A   Set screw.
B   Knurled knob for making lateral adjustments. The Vernier scale shows the sight set at 'zero'.

THE VERNIER SCALE. The main scales on aperture sights are graduated in divisions .05 in. apart, each division representing five minutes of angle. The vernier scale, for reading measurements smaller than five minutes, is graduated in divisions .04 in. apart. Thus, in a total of twenty minutes, there will be four five-minute divisions on the main scale and five four-minute divisions on the vernier scale. The vernier is defined as a moving scale for obtaining fractional parts of the sub-divisions of a fixed scale. Some aperture sights, however, have a fixed vernier and a movable main scale.

The arrangement of the lateral and elevation scales on a modern aperture backsight are clearly shown in figures 28 and 30. The elevation scale in increments of hundreds of yards is also shown in figure 28, and the method of reading the vernier scale in terms of minutes in figure 31.

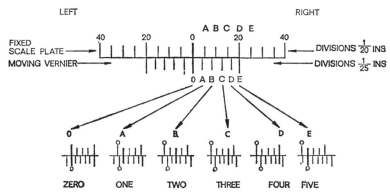

Fig. 31. The Vernier scale and how to read it.
Moving the eye-piece to the right 1 minute (2 clicks) brings A opposite A.
Moving the eye-piece to the right 2 minutes (4 clicks) brings B opposite B.
Moving the eye-piece to the right 3 minutes (6 clicks) brings C opposite C.
Moving the eye-piece to the right 4 minutes (8 clicks) brings D opposite D.
Moving the eye-piece to the right 5 minutes (10 clicks) brings E opposite E.
Zero (0) on the moving scale plate will now have moved in line with (E) on the fixed scale, indicating a 5-minute movement to the right.

MAKING SIGHT ADJUSTMENTS. Elevation adjustments are made by turning the knob on top of the sight; lateral adjustments by the knob on the end of the horizontal arm. The appropriate knob is turned in a clockwise direction to raise the elevation and vice-versa to lower it. Turning the lateral adjustment knob in a similar manner will move the eyepiece to the right or left respectively.

The eyepiece must be moved in the same direction as it is desired to move the position of the group on the target. Thus, to raise the position of the group, the elevation must be raised. Similarly, moving the sight to the right brings the group to the right and vice-versa.

It should be remembered that, regardless of the position of

the eyepiece, the line of sight remains constant—the axis of the bore, and therefore the line of projection, varying in angle to the line of sight according to the vertical and lateral position of the eyepiece.

CARE IN SIGHT SETTING. In the backsights already described, a half-minute click should move the eyepiece .005 in. in the desired direction and a quarter-minute click should move it half that amount. Such small increments are difficult to maintain and, as wear develops in a sight, errors are inevitable. Backlash —when the eyepiece fails to respond to knob movement—is a common fault, generally found in sights that have had a fair amount of usage. When backlash exists, the first one or two clicks may produce no movement and further turning of the sight knob will be necessary to move the eyepiece. In these circumstances, it will be necessary to read the sight scale for each adjustment to ensure that the correction has been made. A sight in this condition can cause considerable confusion to the firer and it should be rectified or replaced without delay. A member of a coached team should always have his sights in good condition so that he can make sight corrections to comply with the coach's wind call whilst still maintaining his aim. If he has to come off aim and fiddle with his sight because of backlash. he will find it irksome, tiring and time consuming and render the coach's task more difficult (chapter 14, Team Shooting and Tie Shooting).

FORESIGHTS. For many years only the standard blade type military foresight was permitted for competition shooting, though limited departures from the 'as issued' type were allowed in later years. Broad foresights with 'streamlined' blades to give sharper definitions were used, and undoubtedly helped shooters with defective vision.

Since the introduction of the 7.62 mm Target Rifle, most restrictions on foresights have been removed and they may now take any form including blades, rings with round or square apertures, cross-wires etc. They may be made of metal or other opaque material or be in the form of transparent discs of any colour with rings, lines etc. inscribed upon them. Tunnels or shades must not exceed 60 mm in length or 35 mm in diameter.

Under N.R.A. rules only the Service Rifle in its 'as issued' condition may be used in Service Rifle target shooting and the standard military foresight is a blade or parallel post. This type of foresight superseded the 'barleycorn' (broader at the base than at the tip) on the S.M.L.E. Rifle in 1907 and was the only type of foresight allowed in British full-bore target shooting until the introduction of the Target Rifle. Although in use for many years in .22 in. target shooting, ring foresights were first allowed under N.R.A. rules in 1968. They have many advantages over blade foresights—on which there are now no restrictions as to width—and are especially helpful to those whose eyes are no longer young.

The modern Target Rifle foresight assembly consists of a tube or tunnel mounted on the barrel. Foresight 'elements' are inserted in the tube and firmly held in position by a locking sleeve. The metal type of elements have projecting lugs which fit into corresponding slots in the tunnel. The transparent variety are not usually positioned in this way and are therefore generally only used for ring foresights with circular apertures. If lines are marked on such elements, a more positive method of positioning is necessary. There is a wide variety of types and sizes of ring foresight elements (figure 32). Full details of their use will be found in chapter 9.

Fig. 32. Metal foresight elements which may be used on the target rifle. The ring element is generally the most popular

ZEROING. Zeroing is the process of ensuring that the line of sight is in correct relationship to the line of projection.

A rifle is considered to be correctly zeroed laterally when the mean point of impact (m.p.i.) of a group of shots strikes the vertical centre-line of the target, with the zero lines on the windage scale-plate coincident. The only departure from this—as explained later in this chapter—is when a rifle is specifically zeroed for long range shooting and a small allowance is made for the drift of the bullet.

Zeroing for elevation consists of setting the sights to read 'zero'—or some equally positive reading such as +5—when set to the correct elevation for 200 yards. Zeroing can be carried out on any short range, preferably not in excess of 200 yards. Special zeroing ranges are sometimes available. Differences in holding, aiming, etc, between individuals, make it essential that each marksman should zero his own rifle.

ZEROING RANGES AND TARGETS. A zeroing range should be constructed so that the distance from the muzzle of the rifle to the target is 71 feet 7 ins. At this distance a true minute of angle subtends ¼ inch on the target.

The targets normally used on zeroing ranges are long and narrow with a black circular aiming-mark near the bottom and a vertical line extending upwards from the top of the aiming-mark. When viewed through the sights it should give the appearance of a 200 yards target at that distance. A long range zeroing target is similar but, of necessity, longer, the aiming-mark giving the appearance of a long range target as seen through the sights (figure 33).

On the short range zeroing target the vertical line should be marked appropriately with calculated m.p.i. for ranges up to 600 yards, i.e. 200, 300 and 500, and for 900 and 1,000 yards on the long range target. At the top of the target should be a lateral scale marked in minutes of angle each side of the centre line, for calculating the effect of lateral sight corrections.

METHOD OF ZEROING. Zeroing should be done on a calm day in steady light, using only ammunition of known good quality, as follows:

1. Ensure that the target when fixed to its support is perfectly upright. Check with a plumb-line.
2. If the target is not exactly perpendicular it is impossible to check whether the backsight is upright.
3. For additional steadiness when firing, the forearm or wrist should be supported on a sandbag or similar rest. On no account should the rifle itself be so supported as this would probably affect the normal vibrations of the barrel and the angle of jump.
4. Place the telescope to permit its use without altering firing position.
5. With the sight set at 300 yards and the lateral scale at zero, carefully fire three shots. The shot holes on the target should be cutting each other. If they do not, and there is no reason to suspect any mechanical fault such as a loose sight, fire three more shots. A rifle should not scatter shots at this distance. Setting the sight at 300 yards rather than

at 200 is recommended in order to avoid distorting the aiming-mark with shot holes and making aiming more difficult.

6. Through the telescope determine the group centre, mentally convert the distance from the vertical centre line into minutes of angle, and make such sight adjustments as are necessary to centralise the group. Fire further check groups and make necessary sight adjustments until satisfied that the m.p.i. is exactly on the vertical line.

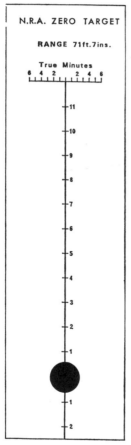

Fig. 33. N.R.A. zero target.

Fig. 34. Evidence of a leaning sight from shots on a zeroing card.

7. To ascertain uprightness of backsight, raise the elevation to 600 yards and fire another two or three shots. The m.p.i. of these should be on or very near to the vertical line.

8. If the lower group is on the centre-line and the upper one is off centre (figure 34), either the firer is leaning his rifle, or the sight itself is leaning, in the direction of the error. Repeat 7 and, if possible, get somebody to check whether the rifle is being held perfectly upright. If the error is repeated when the rifle is known to be upright, a note should be made of the lateral error in terms of minutes so that the necessary allowance can be made when shooting at 500 and 600 yards, on the assumption that the short range zero is correct. This should be regarded as a temporary expedient and the sight should be rectified by a gunsmith or armourer.

9. The same procedure should be adopted for zeroing a rifle for long range shooting except for checking uprightness of sight when the elevation should be set at 1,000 yards. When zeroing a rifle exclusively for long range shooting, 'drift' must be allowed for. When zeroing a 7.62 mm rifle with right-handed rifling twist the sight should be set at at 900 yards and the correct m.p.i. should be $\frac{1}{4}$ in. to the left of the vertical line. With left-handed rifling twist— such as in the .303 in. Lee-Enfield—the m.p.i. should be the same distance to the right.

When a rifle is used mainly at short ranges and only occasionally at long, it is better to have à central zero and make an approximate allowance of one-minute in the required direction when shooting at 900 or 1,000 yards. Ideally, a slight 'lean' on the sights in the desired direction will take care of drift progressively, but this is not always easy to achieve.

10. The elevation markings on a zeroing target should be regarded only as useful guides; final determination of elevation requirements being confirmed at the appropriate ranges.

ZEROING AT LONGER DISTANCES. A rifle *can* be zeroed at longer distances, but not effectively beyond 200 yards. Beyond 200 yards, zeroing is not a practical proposition owing to the effect of wind.

When no proper zeroing range is available, and a marksman has no choice other than 200 yards, ideal conditions are imperative, i.e. a steady light and little or no wind. As he will not be able to carry out the sight uprightness test, he should have this checked mechanically and take the first opportunity of confirming it on a proper zeroing range at the appropriate target.

An advantage of zeroing at 200 yards is that it is being carried out under normal practice conditions and the elevation zero can be checked at the same time.

SETTING THE ZERO PLATES. When the rifle is shooting to a true lateral zero, ensure that the two zero marks on the sight scale and plate are coincident (figure 30). If necessary, slacken the scale plate screws, move the plate to the required position and hold it firmly in place while the screws are tightened. When zeroing at 200 yards, and the correct elevation for this range determined, set the range scale plate so that the '0' coincides with the '2' (representing 200 yards) on the elevation scale.

LOSS OF ZERO. In normal circumstances a rifle should maintain its sight zero settings for a reasonable period—certainly for the duration of one shooting season, unless the rifle is re-bedded. If a change of zero occurs, either during or at the beginning of a shoot, it is likely to be caused by one or more of the following:

Large and sudden changes.
1. Six-hole eyepiece out of centre (The commonest cause)
2. Broken sight fixing screw.
3. Bent sightarm.
4. Broken or cracked recoil lug on bolt (Cause of large lateral errors in Lee-Enfield type rifles).
5. Fingers on the barrel.
6. Loose foresight (lateral errors).
7. Ill-fitting or loose foresight element.

Small and gradual change of zero.
1. Loose or broken sight fixing screw.
2. Loose scale plate (giving false readings).
3. Movement or warping of the rifle woodwork affecting the bedding or resulting in interference between barrel and fore-end. Shrinking and swelling of the woodwork due to exposure in sun or rain, and careless handling can give similar effect.

Changes of lateral zero should be given careful and immediate attention. If care in maintenance, sightsetting, and pre-shoot rifle check is exercised, they should be of very infrequent occurrence.

POSSIBLE ELEVATION CHANGES. Small elevation changes of up to one-minute at short ranges (200 to 600 yards) and two to three minutes at long ranges (900 and 1,000 yards) can be caused by different light conditions, wind, and the difference between makes and batches of ammunition. With 7.62 ammunition, this latter factor is of considerable importance as wide velocity variations exist between one make and another. A marksman should learn to anticipate them, and to distinguish between the normal small zero changes and the abnormal ones which indicate something of a more serious character.

GROUPING. Good scores are dependent upon the ability of the firer to group the requisite number of shots within the highest possible scoring ring on the target. It therefore follows that, in addition to being sufficiently small to fulfil this requirement, the group must be correctly placed on the target.

A marksman should, from time to time, check his holding ability and the grouping capacity of his rifle. This can best be done by firing groups at 100 yards, though shorter distances may be used. Accuracy testing of Service rifles at ordnance factories is carried out at 30 yards, with additional percentage check shoots at longer distances.

As in zeroing, favourable weather conditions are desirable for grouping tests. Reasonably warm weather is also advantageous as good shooting can seldom be achieved with cold hands and fingers. Grouping can be carried out on a large sheet of plain white card or stiff paper on which are placed black aiming-marks of appropriate size. It is then possible to fire several groups without changing targets. A six-inch mark will generally prove suitable for use at 100 yards. Groups are generally measured in terms of minutes.

Only a limited number of shots can be fired before fatigue begins to reduce accuracy and, if a number of rifles are to be tested, a rest or sandbag may be desirable. If only two or three seven- or ten-shot groups are to be fired at reasonably spaced intervals, the firer may decide to use a sling and conduct his group testing in a manner similar to normal range practice. A gunsmith or armourer group testing a number of rifles in the course of his business would use a rest since his object would be to check the grouping capacity of the rifles and not necessarily his own shooting. Ordnance factory testing is normally carried out from mechanical rests.

A Word of Warning. The number of good shots a well regulated rifle will fire is not inexhaustible and it is futile to waste them on unnecessary groups. Similarly, if too much shooting is done at one time the firer's standard may deteriorate and give a false impression of the weapon's performance. Groups should therefore only be fired when it is essential to determine whether all is well or that something is seriously wrong. Only the best available ammunition should be used for grouping.

GROUP CENTRING AND ERROR CHASING. Retrospective examination of a score-book will often show examples of a shoot spoiled by the firer's inability to appreciate at an early stage exactly where his group was forming. Most of the shots fired may have been in one direction, resulting in the loss of valuable points. And often an early shot has a misleading effect and causes an over-correction which is maintained throughout the shoot.

It must be appreciated that, whatever the rifle and ammunition used, every shot will not go through the same hole. The grouping capacity of firer and rifle must always be considered and corrections must be made in relation to the probable position of the m.p.i. that will form as the shoot proceeds. A full correction made on the position of a single shot, which may prove to be the low shot of the series, or may be the left shot of a group which will develop on the right of it, will inevitably result in excessively high or right shots respectively. In such circumstances, if the elevation is known to be correct for the range, and any wind allowance that has been made is considered reasonably correct, it is better to assume that the group will develop nearer to the desired position than they indicate. If the theoretical m.p.i. is calculated in the light of this conjecture and suitable adjustments made, the resultant group is more likely to be centred in or around the bullseye.

An example of what can happen to a marksman of reasonable competence is given below and illustrated at figure 35(i). In this instance it is assumed that the rifle is correctly zeroed, that he is shooting at 200 yards and that the wind effect is negligible.

1. The first sighter is a low inner, A [figure 35(i)]. Without alteration he fires his second sighter B which is close to A and just in the magpie. The firer decides to make a full correction of $2\frac{1}{2}$ minutes on these two shots thus raising his elevation reading from zero (0) to $2\frac{1}{2}$. This moves his group centre from G.I to G.II.

2. The next two shots 1 and 2 are still low in the group (G.II)

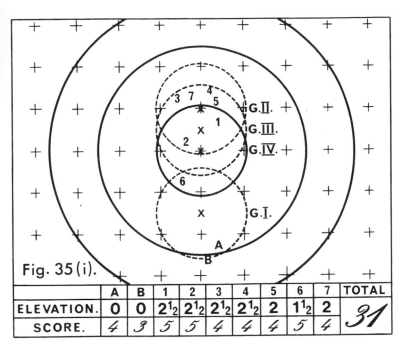

Fig. 35 (i).

	A	B	1	2	3	4	5	6	7	TOTAL
ELEVATION.	0	0	$2\frac{1}{2}$	$2\frac{1}{2}$	$2\frac{1}{2}$	$2\frac{1}{2}$	2	$1\frac{1}{2}$	2	*31*
SCORE.	4	3	5	5	4	4	4	5	4	

and are comfortably within the bullseye and the firer is confident that he has made the correct adjustment.

3. Shot 3 is high though still within the group and is an inner. The firer is not unduly perturbed and fires again, this time getting another high inner which is still within group G.II. This worries him a little and he lowers his elevation a half-minute bringing his group centre to G.III.

4. His next shot (5) is well within G.III group area though a little high and produces another high inner.

5. He is now getting rather desperate and comes down another half-minute bringing his group for the first time to the centre of the bull (G.IV). Shot 6 is a low bullseye which again rattles him somewhat with the result that he regrets his last move and puts back the half-minute losing his last shot at 12 o'clock. Result a very disappointing score of 31.

Let us now consider how the more experienced marksman would have dealt with the situation. See figure 35(ii).

1. His sighters A and B fall in the same place but realising

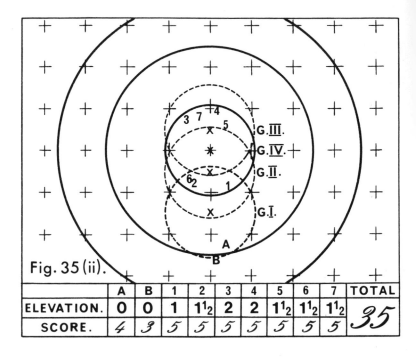

Fig. 35 (ii).

	A	B	1	2	3	4	5	6	7	TOTAL
ELEVATION.	0	0	1	1¹₂	2	2	1¹₂	1¹₂	1¹₂	35
SCORE.	4	3	5	5	5	5	5	5	5	

that his elevation is unlikely to have altered much since his last shoot at 200 yards, he assumes that there are the low shots of a group likely to form at G.I. He therefore proceeds cautiously and raises his sight 1 minute thus moving his group centre to G.II.

2. His first counting shot is comfortably within the group but only just in the bullseye at 6 o'clock. He therefore goes up another half-minute bringing his group to the centre of the bull (G.IV). Shot 2 is again low and worries him a little so he raises his sight another half-minute bringing the group centre to G.III. Shots 3 and 4 are both high. He ignores 3 but feels he must act on 4 so comes down the half-minute bringing his group centre once again to G.IV.

3. His last three shots being within the group area are all bullseyes making his score 35, a 'possible'.

The shoot described is not a particularly good one in any case showing a tendency to 'climb' throughout, possibly due to minor defects in the rifle's bedding or to the firer's visibility problems, but by proceeding carefully a good score could result from it. If on the other hand the corrections made were too drastic the results obtained would be disappointing.

7

FOUNDATIONS OF SUCCESS—
PHYSICAL AND PSYCHOLOGICAL

Active participation in any sport or pastime frequently entails undertaking something difficult to the point of impossibility, within the bounds of a set of rigidly imposed rules—written or unwritten—which make achievement still 'more difficult. Material gain may be little or non-existent, but in the matter of personal satisfaction and enjoyment the participants may consider the rewards beyond price.

Competitive target shooting is such a sport—calling for a high standard of accuracy and precision in repeatedly hitting a small target at long distances. The participant is dependent on his judgement, experience and ability, and the consistent performance of his weapon and ammunition. Because of the importance of the purely human and individual element, however, target shooting can justifiably be described as a test of character.

Many keen shots devote much of their spare time and cash and an inordinate amount of thought to rifle shooting without ever achieving distinction. Some, in fact, seldom appear in the prize lists in competitive shooting and never win anything of note. Yet, in spite of this lack of success, target shooting remains their favourite pastime. Equally dedicated and single-minded are others who, although no more prepossessing than less successful marksmen, achieve a steady measure of distinction in both individual and team events. Finally, there are a comparatively small number in the top class whose consistently high standards have earned them places in international teams and a reputation of being among the elite of target shooters. Yet their equipment is basically the same as the others. How then to explain this ascendency over their rivals? The answer lies in a combination of facets—physical, mental and emotional—the disturbance of any one of which will reveal itself clearly in the results obtained.

THE SUCCESSFUL MARKSMAN. To be successful a marksman should have the full use of his arms, hands, shoulders, and at least the upper half of his body. We make this qualification because there have been instances of men achieving distinction in spite of disabilities such as the loss of one or both legs.

The optical problems are dealt with in Chapter Ten. At this stage it is sufficient to say that keen, unassisted eyesight is a great advantage but by no means a primary essential. Many good shots have worn glasses for much of their lives and probably throughout their entire shooting careers. Normal vision, i.e. neither long nor short-sightedness, is probably an invaluable asset being so much easier to correct when emmetropia (loss of accomodation) attendant upon middle-age makes its inevitable appearance.

Much has been written and said about the need for physical fitness on the range and some enthusiasts go into serious training. In our opinion however, this is not necessary provided that excesses of food, drink and smoking are avoided. A normal diet and daily routine are quite sufficient fortification against the relatively mild exertion and feeling of excitement experienced in any important competitive shoot. Excitement is natural and indeed necessary to inspire the extra effort and concentration required to achieve success. Physical and psychological characteristics vary with the individual and not everyone will possess all the requirements of a first-class shot. However, given reasonable health, average vision and the time to devote to a moderate amount of practice, there is no reason why one should not develop the necessary attributes to become one.

ADDITIONAL REQUIREMENTS FOR FIRST-CLASS MARKSMANSHIP. The successful marksman is prudent and leaves nothing to chance. He is meticulous in his attention to detail, though not to the extent of fussiness. He makes sure that his rifle, or rifles, are in first class order, correctly zeroed, and the sights perfectly upright. Any faults, however small, are quickly dealt with. He endeavours to profit from any previous mistakes, ensuring that a lesson once learned is not forgotten. He avoids stupid blunders such as preparing to shoot on the wrong target or forgetting vital items of equipment, and is ever mindful of disturbing others with whom he may be shooting. And he does his best to develop an imperturbable temperament so that he may deal objectively with any problems that arise.

Some people are born with a phlegmatic disposition, often to the extent that nothing less than an earthquake would disturb their equanimity. These are fortunate in some respects and they often have a soothing effect on their fellow marksmen—but they seldom rise to great heights in marksmanship. In contrast, the excitable person, who is in high spirits one day and despondent the next, can often pull off a wonderful performance. But he is apt to be so temperamental that he can never be relied on for a moderately good shoot. His uncertainty makes him something of a liability in team events when, if things go really badly for him, the morale of the entire team may be affected. Ideally, then, the perfect temperament falls between the two extremes, and the calm unshakable disposition is a virtue developed by careful self-control.

When things go wrong, the person who can view the situation dispassionately will be able to see beyond immediate worries. While still dealing calmly with the situation as it develops, he is able to appreciate that an apparently major set-back may not be as bad as it appears. He keeps calm and steadily fights on for every point right to the end of the shoot.

By far the most important requirement for a first-class marksman is determination. The man who really wants to reach the top must do so by his own efforts. In individual competitions everybody else is out to beat him and, though a very friendly sport, shooting is fiercely competitive. While there is no room for ruthless self-advancement and certainly no sympathy for anyone failing to abide scrupulously by the rules, the man who lacks ambition will seldom make the grade.

CONFIDENCE. To succeed, a marksman must have confidence in his ability and equipment. Normally, good scores do not come easily but are the result of much effort, care and research, though there are rare occasions when everything seems to fall neatly into place. Then a marksman makes his wind assessments with firm decision, sees the sights and aiming-mark with satisfying clarity and fires with confidence. He feels reasonably sure that each shot he fires is a good one and in the bulls-eye. Such occasions happen infrequently, but when they do they should be savoured to the full.

A word of caution though. While confidence is eminently desirable, over-confidence can be positively detrimental as it may detract from that spirit of determination that is so essential to success. Many a young and inexperienced shot has allowed an unexpected run of good scores to colour his judgment of his own ability, attributing his good fortune entirely to skill and overlooking the possibility of 'beginner's luck'. He feels he knows it all, until some lack of care and attention to detail provides a rude awakening.

The disappointments experienced in target shooting are many and varied and the wise marksman learns to bear them philosophically and, above all, avoids boring others with his tales of woe. On the other hand, when success crowns his efforts, he can feel satisfied that this has only been achieved by his determination to win.

WHAT ARE THE REWARDS? From the foregoing it may appear that target shooting is fraught with disappointments, as indeed it is. It is often a physical and mental struggle, and particularly on a hot day and when things go badly one may reach a state of semi-exhaustion. The tangible rewards are few and far between and sometimes never materialise. A good shoot provides a retrospective sense of achievement and satisfaction, though frequently this is marred by the realisation that, though the effort was a good one, it was not quite good enough and somebody else was just a little bit better.

It appears difficult to justify a sport which apparently has so little to offer to its devotees. The fact remains, however, that once a person has become infected with real enthusiasm for target shooting, its fascination usually lasts for life. If he participates in the British National Prize Meeting he will return to Bisley year after year, to meet old friends and make new ones and to continue the struggle against adversity. Even if he does not compete in open prize meetings but is content to confine his activities to his own particular locality the fascination of target shooting will still prevail.

Perhaps its most redeeming feature is that target shooting is a sport one can follow for life. Even though age may dim the eyesight, experience often outweighs this disadvantage. The unexpected, too, often happens. After years of patient unrewarded endeavour, a little luck may suddenly project a marksman to the top of the ladder of fame, to his gratified amazement and the surprise of his friends who may find pleasure in reflecting that it could happen to them too.

The rewards of target shooting are not necessarily material but, for those prepared to make the necessary effort they will almost certainly eventually be forthcoming.

8

FOUNDATIONS OF SUCCESS—
THE PRACTICAL SIDE

THE PRONE POSITION. Since most competitive shooting under N.R.A. rules is conducted with the firer prone on the ground, it is essential that a comfortable and consistent firing position is regularly adopted. Such a position must allow the shooter to fire a long series of shots without fatigue. It must embody a correct and favourable position of the head when aiming and enable maintenance of stability of the rifle without muscle tension or strain.

Military teaching of the prone position required the firer to lie at an angle of approximately 45 degrees to the line of fire, legs widely spaced and heels flat on the ground. For a great many years this position was taught to all marksmen whether civilian or military.

Obviously the civilian target shooter can please himself as regards the postion he adopts and soon develops individual characteristics that suit his build and comfort. While the majority still favour what is basically a traditional prone position, the exaggerated angle to the target and spread of legs has tended to diminish, even if only on account of the limited space on firing points and the inevitable interference with neighbouring shooters. Some marksmen cross their legs at the ankle others by bending the right knee and placing the right instep over the left leg.

In all cases the abdomen is flat on the ground and the rifle supported by the triangle formed by the two elbows and the chest and postioned by the hands, cheek and shoulder.

In recent years with the increasing interest in International shooting and with the consequent pooling of knowledge among competing nations, further developments have been taking place particularly in such countries as the U.S.A. and Russia, both of which have achieved great successes in Olympic and World Championship shooting.

The result is that a different style of prone position has been developed which is claimed to have considerable advantages over the 'conventional' position described above. Its chief features are as follows:—

(1) Angle of the body to line of fire relatively small, 10-15 degrees, the spine and left leg being approximately in line.

(2) The right knee is slightly bent, the leg being drawn up and the foot placed flat on the ground. This is supposed to raise the chest off the ground thus making for easier breathing.

(3) The left arm is placed slightly to the left of the rifle (not underneath it) and ideally if viewed from above, the left arm, left side and left leg should form a straight line. The left foot can be placed with the toe only on the ground or even turned inwards.

(4) The right elbow should be so placed that the shoulders are level, and the head should be as nearly upright as possible so that the aiming eye is looking straight ahead.

(5) The sling is placed round the left arm either above or below the biceps muscle, the theory here being that the pulse in the arm is so avoided.

(6) The rifle rests in the left hand rather than being held, and the grip of the right hand is dependent upon the weight of the trigger pull. The heavier the pull, the tighter the right hand grip.

There is no doubt that some remarkably fine shooting has been done in recent years by users of this new prone position, and while the authors cannot claim to have had much personal experience of it, they recommend the beginner to try it in comparison with what might be called the 'conventional' position, and to adopt it if it suits him. For the confirmed shooter who has had many years of experience with the conventional position, to make the change must be a decision for him alone. He must give it a fair trial however as the first attempt will probably not be a success particularly if at the same time he changes to a single point sling having used the two point variety for many years.

It is emphasised that this new position is basically designed for use with the single point sling and a hand-stop is considered to be necessary as well.

The authors therefore recommend the beginner to experiment a bit before coming to a firm decision. The important thing is to be comfortable, to adopt automatically the same position every time one shoots, and having made a decision one way or the other to stick to it. Changing around every few weeks will achieve nothing. See plates opposite for examples of prone positions.

26

27

Plate 26. The rifle is held and kept in position by the hands, face and shoulder supported by the tripod formed by elbows and chest.

Plate 27. An orthodox prone position. This marksman makes full use of his hat brim to shade his backsight. The telescope is positioned to necessitate minimum head movement.

HOLDING THE RIFLE. Having found and adopted a comfortable and consistent firing position, the next step is to bring the rifle into the shoulder and maintain it there with reasonable steadiness.

Once again, at this stage it should be tried without a sling on the rifle, and practice at home will be particularly helpful. A miniature target, or a small mark on a wall, at which aim can be taken will help to ascertain the correct angle of the body to the line of fire. The target or mark should be placed about 12 inches from the ground and the sight set at a comfortable elevation reading.

To adopt the firing position, all that is now required is to position the butt in the shoulder with the right hand at the same time holding the fore-end with the left hand. The butt should be pressed firmly into the hollow of the shoulder, and the jaw bone brought down into contact with the butt. A good tip is to place the heel of the butt slightly higher than is actually required and then press it down with the side of the face until it reaches the desired spot in the shoulder.

The hold of the right hand is of the utmost importance. A really good grip of the small of the butt is essential for drawing the butt into the shoulder and keeping it there. The finger-tips should press firmly against the butt and the thumb be laid across the top, the whole hand being in such a position as to allow the first joint of the index finger to get well round the trigger. The face should rest against the thumb. The rifle should lie diagonally across the palm of the left hand, the fore-end being held in a firm and positive manner. It must be remembered that a rifle firing a Service calibre cartridge recoils considerably when fired. If not securely held it can deliver some unpleasant knocks. These, if allowed to continue, will inevitably lead to flinching.

More important still is the fact that if a rifle is not under complete control it will seldom produce good scores. It is of interest to watch and compare the behaviour of rifles of known good shots with those of the less experienced. The former, when fired, move backwards in a direct line and with the minimum amount of movement, whereas the latter sometimes describe circular or sideways movements and even collapse in undignified fashion to the ground.

RIFLE SLINGS. Rifle slings are generally made of leather or strong webbing, both materials being durable and unlikely to stretch to any extent.

Webbing slings have leather ends with brass studs for attaching to the rifle swivels, and adjustments are made by means of a sliding buckle. With this type of adjustment it is a good plan to mark the sling with an ink line showing the normal position of the buckle. This saves time and trouble after departures from normal sling tension have been made to compensate for variations in clothing etc.

The permissible maximum width of the sling, under N.R.A. rules, is 2 ins. Slings are generally made in two widths, 1½ and 2 ins., and which is used is entirely a matter of personal preference. Being attached to the rifle at two points, it is generally known as the two-point sling.

Another type has only one attachment to the rifle and is known as the single-point sling. It is much favoured by American and Continental marksmen and by small-bore shooters and is slowly finding favour among marksmen who shoot under N.R.A. rules (plates 28 to 37).

USING THE SLING. Although good shooting can be done without it—and it is good practice to shoot from time to time without its assistance—all competitive shooting under N.R.A. Target Rifle Rules is done with the use of the sling.

In the armed forces the original and basic purpose of the sling was for carrying the rifle, either slung on one shoulder or diagonally across the body. Used thus, it is attached to the rifle by the butt and upper sling swivels. For sniping, and other more advanced forms of military shooting, the lower end is transferred from the butt to the magazine swivel, and it is used to steady the firer's arm. It is in this form that it is invariably used for target shooting.

A military alternative adopted by the British and some of the Commonwealth armed forces for sniping rifles is the American Springfield sling. This comprises leather straps with hooks for adjusting the length. It is attached to the two normal carrying swivels but can quickly be converted into an arm-supporting sling by releasing a pair of hooks and slipping the arm through the loop thus provided. In this form the sling's attachment to the butt swivel is negligible, the attachment to the rifle being that to the upper sling swivel. It is therefore in effect a single-point sling.

There are several methods of using the two-point sling as an aid to holding the rifle. In describing them, it is assumed that the firer is right-handed and, consequently, the sling will be around his left arm. The method generally used and easiest to learn is illustrated on plates 45 to 48 and described here.

1. Hold the rifle with the right hand at the point of balance—the butt resting on the ground—with the sling hanging in a loop underneath.

2. Pass the left arm through the loop from left to right and then bring the hand under and outside the forward end of the sling.

3. Take hold of the rifle with the left hand at the usual position near the point of balance and, with the right hand, push the sling loop as far up under the arm-pit as possible.

These motions can be gone through when the firer is on his knees or sitting, during the process of adopting the prone position. As the prone position is finally assumed, bring the butt into the shoulder with the right hand. This will push the rifle forward and tighten the sling. The sling should now be positioned so that it passes from the upper sling swivel, underneath the back of the left hand, round the wrist, around the upper arm, and back to the rear sling swivel. The effect of the sling should be to pull the rifle back and hold it firmly against the right shoulder. It should be possible to release the right hand from the small of the butt without in any way disturbing the position of the rifle. If this cannot be done, there is something wrong with the tension of the sling.

Another method of using the sling is to arrange it into a loop before putting the left arm (right for left hand shooters) through (plates 49 to 51). This is recommended as it helps to prevent the sling from slipping down the arm. It is also considered by some marksmen to be a safeguard against canting the rifle. It is a little more difficult getting into the sling using this method, and the sling must be lengthened. In any case, the correct length can only be found by a process of trial and error. In order to ensure that the sling lies flat against the hand it should be given a twist when it is attached to the rifle, in the following manner:

1. Attach the front end of the sling to the upper swivel with the outside of the sling towards the rifle.

2. Keeping the outside of the sling against the rifle fore-end, bring the lower end up in the form of a loop when attaching it to the swivel in front of the trigger-guard.

No matter which of these methods is used, the effect will be diminished if the sling tension is not correct. If the sling is too short and difficulty is experienced in getting the butt into the shoulder, the firer will soon find himself in considerable dis-

29

30

Plate 28. A single-point sling, attached to a target rifle.

Plate 29. The loop portion of the sling in position on the arm. A popular type of sling has this loop in the form of a cuff, readily detachable from the remainder.

Plate 30. The sling in position, for firing. Ideally, the left arm should be directly beneath the rifle and left hand pushed farther forward.

comfort. The pressure on the artery in the upper arm will cause unpleasant pulsation and consequent unsteadiness. In addition, undesirable strain is brought to bear on the rifle, possibly resulting in interference between barrel and woodwork. A sling that is too loose is less likely to have an adverse effect on the rifle's accuracy, but it will afford little support for the firer's arm. Apart from serving no practical purpose, it will tend to slide down the arm towards the elbow, causing the firer to fidget and alter his position—probably disturbing his shooting while he tries to get comfortable.

As with most things in target shooting, it is very important to keep everything stable from shot to shot and from one shoot to another, sling tension being no exception. Additional or fewer clothes to meet temperature changes, variations in the slope of the firing-point and changes in position to allow for uneven ground can all affect the sling tension. The firer must make such small adjustments as are necessary to compensate for these factors. A hook or large button sewn on the shooting-coat sleeve, under the arm-pit, will help to keep the sling in the correct place.

EFFECT OF THE SLING ON HOLDING. With the sling in use, the right hand has comparatively more work to do than the left. Aided by the backward pull of the sling, the right hand keeps the butt of the rifle firmly in the shoulder while one finger is engaged in pressing the trigger. A firm grip should be maintained round the small of the butt in such a manner as to allow the first joint, or the fleshy portion between the first and second joints of the trigger finger, to come easily on the trigger to exert pressure without in any way disturbing the grip. The first finger is usually the more sensitive, but there is no objection to using the second. There should be no need for undue force from the right hand to keep the butt firmly against the shoulder though a firm hold is essential, aided by the action of the sling.

Provided the sling is correctly tensioned and positioned, there is no need to grip the rifle as firmly with the left hand as when a sling is not used. The fore-end should lie across the palm of the hand, with the fingers and thumb acting as steadiers. The actual position of the fore-end in the hand will largely depend on the position of the left elbow in relation to the centre-line of the rifle. It is vitally important that the rifle is under the complete control of the firer. Some can achieve this with a relatively light hold with the left hand, others find a stronger hold necessary. But in either event, it should never be gripped to the extent of

31

32

3

34

Plate 31. In the kneeling position, pass the arm through the sling from left to right.

Plate 32. Push the sling as far up under the armpit as possible, holding the rifle with the left hand.

Plate 33. Assuming the prone position with the sling round the arm.

Plate 34. A correctly tensioned sling.

causing muscular discomfort. It should always be remembered that the firer must be as relaxed as possible, both physically and mentally. The temptation to 'take hold' and strain against the sling towards the end of a good shoot should be resisted as it will assurredly lead to unfortunate results. The wearing of a glove, reducing the likelihood of the rifle slipping in the hand, will help to combat the tendency to grip the rifle too tightly.

Whether shooting with or without the sling, the hands must function in exactly the same manner for every shot, and the hold must be maintained until after the bullet has left the barrel. About .0015 of a second elapses between the time the trigger is pressed and the bullet's exit from the muzzle. Any loosening of the hold in that short but important space of time can result in a wide shot.

CANTING. 'Canting' means leaning the rifle so that the sights are not perfectly upright when a shot is fired. It is a common fault—sometimes unwittingly perpetrated by experienced marksmen—and every effort should be made to prevent it (plates 38 and 39).

When aim is taken, the barrel of the rifle is directed at some point above the aiming-mark to allow for the fall of the bullet. When a rifle is canted, however, it is virtually rotated about the line of sight. The line of sight remains constant but the axis of the bore, and consequently the line of departure of the bullet, is directed to one side of the point aimed at. The bullet travels on a course which, if unaffected by other influences such as wind, will increasingly diverge from the course it would have taken had the rifle not been canted. The divergent line, and the consequent error on the target, will naturally be in the direction in which the rifle leans.

THE EFFECT OF CANTING. The consequence of canting is best explained by showing what can happen at 1,000 yards since at this range—the longest normally used in Target Rifle shooting—the effect is greatest. At distances of less than 600 yards the effect is relatively small.

The elevation required for most 7.62 mm cartridges at 1,000 yards is in the region of 40 minutes of angle, which means that the rifle barrel will be pointing at a spot about 33 to 38 feet higher than the point of aim (figure 36). With the various brands of 7.62 mm ammunition such as used in Target Rifle shooting the required elevation is unlikely to differ by more than a few

36

Plate 35. The sling is attached to the upper swivel with the outside of the sling towards the rifle. Keeping it against the fore-end, bring the lower end up in the form of a loop when attaching it to the magazine sling swivel.

Plate 36. The arm is put through the loop and the sling pushed up under the armpit as shown in plate 46.

Plate 37. The firer in position with the sling well up under the arm, and the 'loop' arrangement clearly visible.

37

minutes so that for all practical purposes the effect of cant will be about the same.

Because of group dispersion one cannot lay down definite figures for canted shots but, theoretically, a cant of 6 degrees causes a lateral error on the target at 1,000 yards of about 4½ feet, resulting in a wide outer (figure 37). There will also be a slight loss of elevation but, as this should only be about 3 ins.,

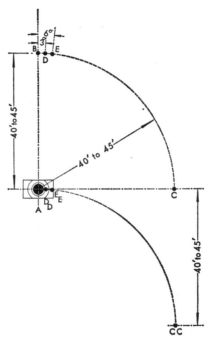

Fig. 36. Effect of canting.

A   Point of aim (centre of target).
B   Point at which the barrel is directed.
C   Point at which the barrel is directed when the rifle is canted 90 degrees to the right.
D   When the rifle is canted to the right 3 degrees.
E   When the rifle is canted to the right 6 degrees.
B—C=   The line on which the barrel will be directed for varying amounts of cant.
A—CC   The line on which the shots may be expected to strike for varying amounts of cant.
DD, EE, CC, represent the strike of shots with 3, 6 and 90 degrees of cant respectively.
A—DD   Lateral error of about 27 inches.
A—EE   Lateral error of about 4.5 feet and vertical error of about 3 inches.

it can be ignored. For a cant of 3 degrees, the error is halved (figure 37) and should result in a wide inner or possibly a magpie.

At 600 yards, canted shots of 6 and 3 degrees will probably produce magpies and inners respectively.

If the canted shots should happen to be the wide ones of the group, and in the direction of the cant, the results could be more serious.

THE EFFECT OF CANT IN A STRONG WIND. Although in normal weather conditions canting errors likely to be made in target shooting have no serious effect on elevation, entirely different circumstances prevail in a strong cross-wind.

When the backsight is adjusted to allow for wind, the eye-piece is moved in the direction from which the wind is blowing. If the rifle is now canted in the opposite direction, the eye-piece will be relatively higher from the centre-line of the bore than in its normal lateral 'zero' position (figure 38). The angle of elevation is increased, the barrel is directed to a slightly higher point on the target, and the shots will go high. For instance, firing at 1,000 yards with the rifle canted 6 degrees to the right and a 20 minute left wind allowance on the backsight, the elevation is increased by about 2 minutes and the shot may be expected to go about 20 ins. high and about $4\frac{1}{2}$ feet to the right. It could, in fact, miss the target altogether. With a 3 degree cant the shot should result in a high magpie. If the rifle is canted into the wind, the eye-piece will be relatively lower (figure 38) and the shot will go low. The lateral error will still be in the direction of the cant.

Therefore, in a strong cross-wind the rule regarding cant is: when the rifle is canted in the same direction as the wind, the shot will go high; when canted against the wind, it will go low.

CAUSES OF CANT AND SUGGESTED REMEDIES. Careless holding, 'tightening-up' and straining for a correct aim are probably the most general causes of cant, and the following can contribute to a greater or less degree:

1. *Astigmatism*—an imperfection of the eye which, in extreme cases, causes irregularity of horizontal and vertical lines. A possible consequence is that the rifle and foresight may appear to lean when they are in fact upright, and vice-versa. The only cure is a corrective eyeglass or lens.
2. *A leaning foresight.* If the foresight is not perpendicular to the barrel, the rifle will be canted slightly in a direction

38   39

40

Plate 38. Canting. Shows an upright rifle with spirit level in position to indicate this. A good method of testing for cant.

Plate 39. Canting. Here the rifle is canted to an angle of 6 degrees.

Plate 40. Partly sheltered Bisley range. The trees and hedgerow on the left of the Century range at Bisley afford a certain amount of shelter to those firing on butt 10 (the left-hand butt) at 500 and 600 yards, when the wind is blowing from the left. Particularly at 600 yards the firers on the left-hand targets usually need appreciably less wind allowance than those further along the firing-point.

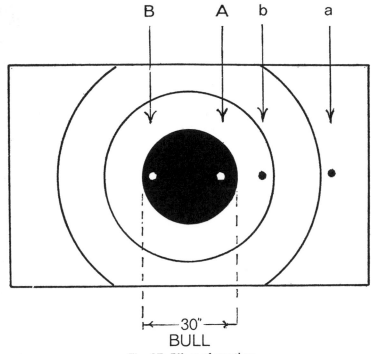

B A b a

|←——30"——→|

BULL

Fig. 37. Effect of canting.

A Where the right-hand shot of a central group could be expected to go.
a Where it would go with a cant of 3 degrees—an outer.
B Where the left-hand shot could be expected to go.
b Where it would go with a cant of 3 degrees—an inner.
Note Only lateral error is shown.

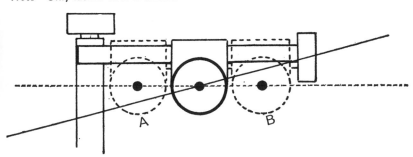

Fig. 38. Canting. The tilted backsight.

A Shows how elevation is increased when allowance is made for wind blowing in the direction of the cant. Shots will go high.
B Shows how elevation is lowered when allowance is made for wind blowing in the opposite direction to the cant. Shots will go low.

opposite to that in which the foresight leans. A change of foresight may effect a cure; but it is more likely to be the foresight-block or block-band which is at fault—a job for an armourer or gunsmith.

3. *A leaning target.* The sides of a target are useful guides for checking that the rifle is upright. If the target leans, however, there will be a tendency to lean the rifle in the same direction. So never fire at a leaning target if it can be avoided. Endeavour to have it straightened.

4. *An uneven firing-point.* On an uneven or sloping firing-point one elbow may be appreciably higher than the other. This can cause a slight cant in the direction of the lower elbow. It is not always possible to avoid slopes and holes, so extra care in holding should be exercised.

The foresight of a correctly held rifle can be likened to the minute-hand of a clock when it points to twelve o'clock (figure 39). At one minute past twelve the minute-hand leans to the right 6 degrees; at five minutes past twelve it leans 30 degrees and so on. Plates 52 and 53 and figure 36 show that a cant of up to 6 degrees is really very small and can easily pass unnoticed by the firer.

CONCLUSIONS. The conclusion arrived at by the late L. R. Tippins—marksman, author and small-arms expert of repute—after many experiments and considerable research on cant are of particular interest. In his book *Modern Rifle Shooting*, published by J. S. Phillips in 1913, describing the effect of cant he states: 'The lean of three degrees is taken because it worked out as the average limit of error of a number of good shots actually firing with the utmost care, only very few men managing to keep their error less than this for a series of ten shots'. Tippins considered that many men did lean their sights as much as six degrees. There is no reason to suppose that his conclusions are not applicable to-day, except that the Target Rifle is more comfortable to hold than the Service Rifles of Tippins' time.

Some marksmen consider that cant does not matter provided the degree of cant is the same for every shot. While this is theoretically true, it is more difficult to determine a precise amount of cant for each shot than it is to ensure an upright rifle. The man who always cants will have a different lateral zero for every range. This causes a troublesome complication, especially to a member of a coached team. A tendency to cant should never be disregarded as it can easily be the cause of wide shots so often blamed on imaginary changes of wind. It can also prove misleading to a team coach. Anyone in doubt about the uprightness of their rifle should get a friend to check them from behind when they are actually shooting.

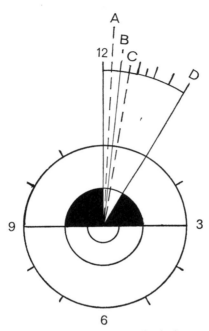

Fig. 39. Canting. Clock face method of assessment.

A   Cant of 3 degrees.   C   Cant of 9 degrees.
B   Cant of 6 degrees.   D   Cant of 30 degrees.

9

FOUNDATIONS OF SUCCESS—
OPTICAL PROBLEMS, AIMING AND
TRIGGER PRESSING

THE EYES. In simple terms, the eyes operate in much the same way as the old-fashioned camera. Reflected light from the object viewed passes through a lens and is transmitted to a sensitive surface behind. By moving the lens backwards or forwards, according to the distance of the object, the image can be sharply defined or, in other words, brought into focus.

The retina—the sensitive surface at the back of the eye—and the pupil are the two most important parts of the eye as far as target shooting is concerned. The ability of the eye to focus, or 'accommodate', is its most important function. Usually in early middle age, due to hardening of the lens and weakening of the eye muscles, the eye loses its ability to focus, particularly nearby objects. This is known as presbyopia.

Long sight (hypermetropia) and short sight (myopia) are conditions which—particularly the former—tend to become more prounounced with advancing age and diminishing power of accommodation. Both, however, are easily rectified from a shooting point of view by the use of spectacles or corrective lenses which fit into the backsight eyepiece. Convex (plus) lenses are used to correct long sight and concave (minus) lenses to correct short sight.

A more complex eyesight defect is astigmatism. This is a condition of the eye in which rays of reflected light from an object are not brought to a focus at one point. It is usually caused by some of the refracting surfaces of the eye being irregular rather than spherical, thus interfering with the eye's ability to focus. Cylindrical lenses are used for the correction of simple astigmatism, and sphero-cylindrical lenses for combinations of astigmatism and long or short-sightedness.

Measurement of lens strength is in dioptres—a dioptre representing a lens with a focal length of one metre. Lenses are ground to give increments in strength of quarter dioptres, e.g. a moderately strong plus lens for a long-sighted person might be +1.5 dioptres while a short sight correction might need a lens of—.75 dioptres. Astigmatism correction is described in degrees right or left.

It is not intended to go into abstruse technical details on eyes and their correction, but it is useful for a marksman to have a rough idea about the cause of eyesight difficulties. And at the first suspicion of faulty eyesight he should seek professional advice.

THE ACTION OF THE EYE WHEN AIMING. A normal aim is taken by looking through the centre of the eyepiece aperture, focusing the eye on the foresight and aligning it with some determined point on the target, usually the aiming-mark.

To the young shot with keen eyesight aiming is usually a simple procedure, the foresight and aiming-mark both standing out with satisfactory clarity. The young eye, with full power of accommodation, can rapidly change its focus from foresight to aiming-mark, and vice-versa, so that both are sharp and clear. As the eyes get older, however, they lose their power of accommodation. The ability to focus diminishes with the result that the foresight appears blurred and its hazy outline tends to merge with the equally hazy aiming-mark.

When it is realised that an aiming error of one-fiftieth of an inch in the relative positions of foresight and aiming-mark leads to a displacement on the target of 15 ins. at 600 yards, it is obvious that the foresight must be sharply focused—even at the expense of clarity of the target. With a sharply defined foresight, however hazy the aiming-mark, an error of this magnitude is unlikely to be made without being noticed by the firer.

This problem is aggravated when a blade foresight is used. For the marksman with failing eyesight it eventually becomes a continual problem experimenting with various thicknesses of foresight and lenses of different strengths while trying to establish a satisfactory combination.

The situation has now been vastly improved by the introduction of ring foresights for full-bore shooting. These have long been in use in other countries and for small-bore shooting. They have never previously been permitted under N.R.A. Rules— except in conjunction with the optical sights used on long range Match Rifles (chapter 15).

With the circular black aiming-marks now used at all distances, the optical problems have largely been overcome, and the shooter is able to choose a ring foresight of suitable aperture for any particular range, or a blade of suitable thickness if he perfers this to a ring.

THE USE OF LENSES AND SPECTACLES. To those with short sight, wearing spectacles is probably something to which they have become so accustomed that it presents no problem, and the glasses they normally use may be quite suitable for target shooting without further correction.

The long-sighted person, however, who has probably never thought that he may someday need optical aid is generally unaware of the onset of presybopia—at any rate as far as it affects his shooting. He can still see clearly targets, wind-flags, score book, and read his sight scales without much difficulty, though his foresight—that vital aid to aiming—is not in sharp focus. If he uses a blade, this will almost certainly lead to deterioration in his shooting, with vertical errors predominating. With a ring forsight the effect may not be as serious and, in fact, may not be experienced at all. Even so, some degree of optical correction will eventually become necessary and necessitate a visit to an optician who will be able to prescribe a suitable lens.

Lenses for the correction of astgimatism are suitably marked to indicate their 12 o'clock position in the backsight eyepiece. It is of vital importance that the mark on the lens is always in its correct position and it must face the firer's eye. If reversed, it will alter the axis of astigmatic correction. Similarly, as the firer's head is slightly tilted when aiming, the correct position for the lens mark will probably be between twelve and one o'clock. Lenses are liable to work loose and move in their holders thus neutralising the astigmatic correction so they should frequently be checked for position.

Eye piece lenses have the advantage of being largely un-affected by rain, body heat etc., though care must be taken not to breathe on them when coming into the aim.

The short-sighted marksman will probably have his optical correction in the form of spectacles. In many ways these are preferable to eyepiece lenses as they are always at a fixed distance from the eye—a matter of some importance with strong lenses. Also, being in position throughout a shoot, they are more restful to the eyes. For eyes that require it a bi-focal segment can be incorporated enabling a firer to read his sight scales, make entries in his score-book etc., without having to remove his spectacles or resort to the use of a magnifying glass.

Certain optical deficiencies, particularly astigmatism, may be more efficiently corrected by the use of contact lenses. If this is the case, the wearer has a considerable advantage over those who have to rely on normal spectacles or eyepiece lenses. In wet weather spectacle lenses are very difficult to keep dry and in hot, humid conditions become steamed up. With contact lenses, these problems are completely eliminated, and the wearer may even enjoy better vision than would be the case with more conventional optical correction.

Contact lenses are only suitable for certain types of eye and optical error, and are therefore only applicable to a limited extent. In any case, a rifleman considering the use of such lenses should consult an optician who specialises in this field and should make his requirements quite clear. The optician can then decide whether or not contact lenses will meet his needs.

The authors do not claim any personal or first-hand knowledge on this particular subject, but feel that this work would be incomplete if mention was not made of this modern optical development.

COLOURED FILTERS. Coloured filters are circular, optically-ground glass discs. They are obtainable in a variety of colours and are designed to fit the various types of eye-pieces and lens holders.

The main object of a filter is to reduce the glare of reflected light from the target and its immediate surroundings, particularly in bright sunlight. It is also helpful, in certain colours, for sharpening up the definition of the target and aiming-mark on dull, hazy days, It is difficult to recommend any one colour as being superior to others, but probably the most versatile is yellow. Not only does it reduce glare on bright days but it is, without doubt, the best for penetrating haze and for defining the target against a dark background. Other helpful colours are medium green and blue, the latter being particularly useful in countries like Africa and Australia where the sunshine is brilliant.

The actual choice of filter is a matter for the individual. One will find that some colours are more beneficial than others under certain conditions, and it is therefore advantageous to possess more than one filter. Many shooters carry a small collection in their shooting bags or cases, ready for any eventuality.

LENS HOLDER EYEPIECES. There are several types of lens-holder eyepieces for use with target rifle backsights: a simple type consisting of an eyepiece with removable flange with an internal recess into which the filter is placed before it is screwed back into position. One of the best of all types is the Steward lens-holder which caters for both correcting lens and filter. In this the lens can be placed in the main recess and a removable cap is available for a filter which can be screwed on or off as desired (figure 49, chapter 12).

Fig. 40. Iris eyepiece.

The iris de luxe-type eyepiece with built-in variable filters is excellent for indoor shooting or for use in hot dry conditions but it is not recommended if there is any risk of rain to interfere with visibility.

FORESIGHTS. The extension of the N.R.A. rules governing target shooting to permit the use of the ring foresight as well as the blade, and the adoption of the circular black aiming-mark for all ranges, undoubtedly benefits the older marksmen. It enables them to continue to shoot well even though past the age when failing eyesight begins to take its toll. Ring foresights have been in use in other parts of the world, and universally by small-bore marksmen, for many years. It is, however, a new departure in United Kingdom and Commonwealth target rifle shooting to use them at long ranges, except in the sighting systems on Match Rifles (chapter 15 on Match Rifle shooting).

Small-bore shooting seldom takes place beyond 100 metres and most Continental full-bore shooting is conducted at 300 metres. In each case the size of the aiming-mark used is sufficiently large to facilitate the use of ring foresights but if these aiming-marks were enlarged proportionally to subtend the same relationship in minutes of angle at greater distances, they would be far too large for satisfactory reproduction on the normal sized targets. It therefore follows that the aiming-marks used for target rifle shooting must be something of a compromise between what is desirable and what is practicable.

A marksman must therefore decide whether to use a ring or a blade type of foresight and, if the former, the size and thickness of the ring he finds most suitable. To add to the problem, if a lens is required for optical correction its strength must be such as to give reasonably sharp definition of the foresight while still allowing the firer to see the aiming-mark clearly. Inevitably, this entails a good deal of experiment by trial and error and, to facilitate this, tunnel type foresights are in general use. Besides allowing easy exchange of foresight elements, they shade the ring or blade from the effect of sun and rain.

With the old Service type of foresight it was a relatively complicated matter to exchange foresight blades and each change almost certainly necessitated re-zeroing the rifle. In consequence, a change of foresight—which could have been the answer to many a shooter's problem—was often deferred because of the other issues involved. The advantage of the inter-changeable type is therefore obvious. It is emphasised, however, that the ease with which foresights can be changed should not lead to indiscriminate changing. Once a satisfactory formula has been worked out, it should be adhered to as far as possible.

BACKSIGHT, SIZE OF APERTURE. The precise size of backsight aperture to give the best results is largely one of personal pre-ference. The deciding factor is the old problem of focusing the foresight, and the choice of size must be closely related to this vitally important point.

The Service type backsight, as used in Service Rifle shooting, has a fixed size aperture of 0.1 in. diameter, which is normally considered to be too large for accurate target shooting but satisfactory for active service purposes.

The Target Rifle marksman can use any size of aperture he likes, and eyepieces with apertures of different sizes are available for his use. The size of aperture can be altered easily and quickly, even in the firing position, and the ideal size to suit the eye under the prevailing conditions of light and visibility can be selected and used. The normal variable aperture eyepiece has six holes, usually differing by 0.005 in. diameter and ranging from 0.04 in. to 0.065 in. An even greater range can be obtained with the iris diaphragm type of eyepiece (figure 40), which has the advantage of being concentric—whereas the six-hole type can, if care is not taken, be out of centre. An off-centre eyepiece can have a devastating effect on a shoot. With an iris diaphragm there is a danger of accidental alteration of aperture, particularly when the rifle is covered by the firer between shots in wet weather.

It is advisable to use the smallest possible aperture commen-surate with a sharply focused foresight, though not so small as to cause a loss of light and consequent strain on the eye.

The size of aperture most commonly used under normal light conditions in the United Kingdom is about 0.05 in. This is large enough to give a clearly defined foresight and yet small enough to give a warningly blurred 'sight picture' should the eye stray from its position of correct alignment. It will probably be necessary to use a larger size in very dull light, particularly at the longer distances where the target and aiming-mark are less clearly defined. In bright light, one size smaller than that normally used is often beneficial.

THE EYE AND THE BACKSIGHT. The relationship between the eye and the backsight aperture is of primary importance in aiming. The ideal is achieved when the eye, the centre of the aperture, the foresight and the point of aim are all in line. In this position the maximum of light passes through the aperture, giving the clearest picture of the foresight and the target. Immediately the eye moves from this line of sight, the available light diminishes, giving a correspondingly less clear picture. And the further the eye wanders from the centre, the more blurred the picture becomes. The eye should be as close to the eyepiece as comfort and safety from recoil will permit. An uncomfortable position will induce neck strain and may impair vision by restricting the normal blood supply to the head. A cut nose or damaged spectacles from the effect of recoil could cause gun-shyness which, in turn, would induce a marksman to anticipate the shock of recoil—with disastrous effect on his holding and trigger pressing. The ideal distance, once found, should be constant for every shot.

AIMING. The three most important factors in aiming are:
1. The aiming eye must be positioned so that it looks through the centre of the backsight aperture.
2. Through the aperture, the eye must see the foresight in the same relative position to the target for every shot.
3. The aim must be in correct alignment the moment the final pressure is applied to the trigger, and the alignment must be maintained until the bullet has left the barrel.

In aiming, it is usual to close the non-aiming eye. When difficulty is experienced in keeping this eye closed, an eye shade may be helpful. It is far better, however, and more restful to the vision to shoot with both eyes open. This can be achieved by wearing a wide-brimmed hat with the brim tied down to obstruct the vision of the non-aiming eye.

AIMING WITH A BLADE FORESIGHT. With a blade foresight, aim can be taken at any point on the target—or even off the target, if desired—the distance between the point of aim and the centre

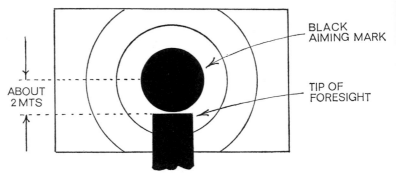

BLACK
AIMING MARK

TIP OF
FORESIGHT

ABOUT
2 MTS

Fig. 41. Aiming with a blade foresight. The six o'clock aim. 1,000 yards target.

of the target being calculated in minutes of angle and the necessary allowance made on the backsight.

What is generally known as the 'six o'clock' aim is largely used in target shooting with aperture sight and blade foresight. The tip of the foresight is aligned at the lowest centre portion of the aiming-mark, with a narrow strip of target showing between foresight and aiming-mark (figure 41). The actual width of the narrow strip of target can be determined only by the firer to suit his particular vision. This aim is probably the best, particularly for the beginner, but it can be difficult to maintain in certain light conditions—especially when the targets are in the shade and the sun in the firer's eyes, and in the evening when the sun is low in the sky.

For many years the flat based tin-hat aiming-mark was used for ranges up to 600 yards. This was admirably suited to the blade foresight, though in poor visibility most people suffered some difficulty in obtaining a clearly defined sight picture, particularly at 600 yards. In Australia, the circular aiming-mark has been used at all distances for many years but, even there where the light is better and clearer than in the United Kingdom, most marksmen experienced problems in maintaining a constant elevation.

The effect of this loss of definition is usually the foresight getting 'lost' in the black aiming-mark, resulting in high shots. Attempts to overcome this by white dots or lines painted on the foresight were permitted in Australia, but not in the United Kingdom. A broad foresight which contrasted well with the curved base of the aiming-mark has been successfully used, and some shooters have obtained good results by covering part, or almost all of the aiming-mark with the foresight.

Fig. 42. The sight picture. Aiming with a ring foresight.

It is reasonable to say that if a marksman has to resort to such methods, he will be much better off using a ring foresight, which is now permitted in most countries.

AIMING WITH THE RING FORESIGHT. The principle of aiming with a ring is basically the same as with a blade. The firer looks through the centre of the backsight aperture and aligns the aiming-mark in the centre of the foresight ring. It possesses the advantage of an 'all round the aiming-mark' sight picture (figure 42). By this means a very exact aim is possible—so exact in fact that every minor error in holding the rifle is discernible to the firer.

With a blade, the foresight must be focused sharply and, as mentioned earlier, suitable lenses may be necessary to ensure this, often to the detriment of clarity of aiming-mark. With a ring foresight however, a certain amount of compromise is possible and, while the foresight must be clearly seen, this can be achieved without diminished clarity of the aiming-mark. A long-sighted person will find that he can see both foresight and aiming-mark clearly using considerably less plus (magnifying) correction than was needed with a blade. On the other hand, a short-sighted marksman may not enjoy quite the same benefit as he must inevitably use a certain amount of optical correction in order to see the aiming-mark at all. One consolation for him, however, is that with advancing years short-sighted vision tends to 'lengthen', i.e. to approach more nearly to normal. He should therefore require progressively less correction whereas long-sighted marksmen should need progressively more.

SIZE OF FORESIGHT RING. This is an important and controversial subject and one to which smallbore marksmen have given much thought over the years. The problem for the full-bore shooter has been complicated by the fact that several changes in diameter of aiming marks have taken place since the use of ring foresights was approved by the N.R.A. and while these have all been directed towards improving the situation, they have made it difficult to do more than generalise on the subject of ring sizes.

At the present time the size of aiming mark at 500 and 600 yards is as large as can conveniently be superimposed on a six-foot target, viz. 36 in. This diameter subtends approximately six minutes of angle, and whilst this is somewhat less than U.I.T. dimensions, it is adequate for all normal purposes. At distances less than 600 yds the same scale applies. At long ranges it is 40 in. which subtends approximately 4 minutes of angle at 1,000 yds.

In addition to the size of foresight aperture, there is also the question of the thickness of the ring itself which has considerable bearing on the degree of optical 'comfort' achieved by the shooter.

Too small a ring which fits the aiming mark snugly can create the impression of a rock-steady aim because minor errors in centralising the black are not noticeable. Also there is risk of optical illusions which seem to have the effect of moving or distorting the aiming mark with disastrous results. It is better to err on the side of having the aperture too large. Errors can readily be seen but there is also a danger of snatching a shot away when the picture 'looks right'. Some shooters go to the extent of having extremely large thick rings with which they encompass the entire target. This seems to be particularly effective at long ranges.

Changes of ring size should, where possible, be avoided as, whilst tunnel foresights are made to reasonably precise limits, small positioning errors are always a possibility and an error of as little as half a minute in position of group can cause the loss of two or three points before the error is discovered. The present bullseye dimensions are too small to allow for such errors. Most shooters manage to find a size of foresight that will suit all distances up to 600 yards. This can at best be regarded as a compromise but is probably preferable to making continual changes. Iris adjustable foresights are now available, and these though somewhat expensive, enable foresight aperture size to be changed easily without affecting the position of the aperture.

While most shooters use round apertures as these seem to be most harmonious within a series of concentric circles, a few pioneers have tried using a square aperture. Both the authors have done so with success and recommend it to those who are not entirely at ease with the round variety.

To lay down hard and fast rules as to size of aperture and thickness of ring would in the opinion of the authors be wrong as so much depends on individual eyesight and attitude of mind. In general however, they would recommend that the shooter uses the largest aperture with which he feels comfortable, uses thick rings rather than thin and having found a satisfactory combination, sticks to it and gets himself thoroughly familiar with it. Constant changing will get him nowhere. If all else fails, try a square aperture or even revert to a very thick blade.

In conditions of poor light, rain or haze, the aiming-mark is frequently very hard to define and sometimes completely disappears. If this occurs, the firer should take drastic action such as using a larger ring, even large enough to encompass the entire target, or possibly changing to a blade.

TRIGGER PRESSING. Trigger pressing, or trigger release, is a particularly important physical factor connected with shooting. Most people can hold a rifle and align the sights to comparatively close limits, but frequently the whole effect is spoiled by faulty trigger release. To get consistent results, trigger release must be accomplished without disturbing the aim.

All military rifles and a high proportion of target rifles require two distinct pressures to be applied to the trigger before the firing mechanism is released. This is a safety measure to prevent accidental discharge. Most small-bore and some full-bore target rifles are fitted with single stage triggers which allow no safety margin of movement before release. To the average target shooter it matters little which type of trigger mechanism is fitted. If he has more than one rifle, however, and they are fitted with different trigger mechanisms, he must always remember which type he is using. Obviously, disaster will result if he attempts to take up the first pressure on a rifle with a single stage pull.

When there are two pressures, the first should be taken when the sights are being aligned on the target and before the commencement of the final aim. As the aim is developed, a steady squeeze using the whole hand and not just the trigger finger should be applied to the trigger and to the small of the butt. The action can be likened to squeezing the water out of a sponge. The final decisive pressure is applied when the aim is exactly right. Constant practice will develop the ability to apply and sustain this steadily increasing pressure.

Some marksmen prefer a more definite 'pull' to a steady squeeze for the final trigger release. This method may be success- ful for those who have, or imagine they have, a rock-like hold that ensures an undisturbed aim. It is not recommended for the beginner and the majority of successful shots use the 'squeeze' technique. The pistol-grip type butts now permitted on target rifles makes holding the rifle far more comfortable than was the case with the Service type of butt. This added comfort should not however, tempt the firer to make the mistake of relaxing his hold with his trigger hand. The grip with this hand is of vital importance. Whatever method of trigger pressing is adopted, the firer must have complete control of the trigger at all times and know exactly how much pressure can be applied with safety. This is one of the most important requirements in accurate target shooting. While a marksman *should* know when his rifle is about to fire, it is *absolutely essential* for him to know with certainty when it is not.

Breathing and the Final Aim. Breathing can have considerable influence on the attainment of a perfect aim.

Immediately prior to the final aim, deep breathing has a steadying effect and helps to alleviate tension and over-anxiety. A deep breath should be taken as the final aim commences. Filling the lungs causes the foresight to go down; then, as the air is gradually expelled, the foresight rises again to the point of aim. The breath can then be held easily and without effort while the aim is perfected and the final trigger pressure is applied.

If the aim starts to deteriorate as the final pressure on the trigger is about to be made, the aim should be immediately relaxed. A further period of deep breathing should be indulged in and a fresh aim commenced. The first exact aim is always the best one. To sustain an aim and restrict breathing in an effort to recapture the same picture tires the eye, builds up a state of tension and inevitably leads to errors in aiming and trigger pressing. It is far better to unload and start again with a fresh, cool cartridge in the chamber.

WIND AND WEATHER

WIND. Wind is air in motion, and it presents a complex problem to marksmen. Whereas the resistance of air to a bullet is more or less constant and can be calculated with reasonable accuracy, the effect on a bullet of moving air is much more difficult to assess.

Wind moves from any point of the compass and is constantly and often rapidly changing in strength and direction. It may be diverted or divided by obstacles in its course, so that currents are actually moving in several directions at the same time— sometimes over relatively small areas of ground such as rifle ranges. Examples of this can be seen on the N.R.A. ranges at Bisley, where hills, hedgerows and belts of trees cause frequent directional changes.

THE EFFECT OF WIND. The effect of wind on a bullet in flight depends on the following factors:
1. The force of the wind.
2. The direction from which the wind is blowing in relation to the path of the bullet.
3. The time the bullet is in the air—which is relative to its speed and the distance it has to travel.

Wind blowing at an angle to the bullet's course will carry the bullet in the direction towards which the wind is blowing. Similarly, wind blowing in the same direction as the bullet will hasten it on its journey, and wind blowing from the opposite direction will retard its flight. Even currents of air rising or falling will have some effect, but only at the longer ranges; and, in any case, they are practically impossible to assess. The effect of a cross wind on a bullet depends upon:
1. The speed or force of the wind.
2. The range.
3. The delay, caused by air resistance, over the distance the bullet has to travel.

The lateral deflection of a bullet due to a cross wind is approximately proportional to distances for ranges up to 600 yards but not beyond. Thus, with a wind blowing at the same strength and in the same direction all over the range, if an allowance of 2 minutes is needed at 300 yards, 4 minutes will be required at 600 yards.

When 'aiming-off' for wind as in Service Rifle shooting the position is complicated by the fact that a minute of angle sub-tends a different amount on the target at each range. Thus, with wind requiring 2 minutes of lateral deflection at 300 yards, an aim-off of 6 ins. will be required. At 600 yards with the same wind which would require an allowance of 4 minutes, 24 ins. of aim-off will be needed—four times as much. In other words, the aim-off expressed in terms of inches varies as the square of the range. Wind however, is seldom constant in strength and direction over a large area, and strictly proportional allowances rarely practicable.

For distances beyond 600 yards, lateral deflection is relatively greater, the bullet being in the air and therefore subjected to the force of the wind for relatively longer periods. The bullet is also losing velocity more rapidly and is therefore more susceptible to the effect of wind.

WIND JUDGING. In judging the force of wind, a marksman has no measuring instruments at his disposal and therefore must rely on visual assessment. This presents a problem for which there is no easy formula and no substitute for experience. Wind can be felt and its effect can be seen, but an estimate of its strength and direction at any given moment can at best be only approximate. While experienced marksmen are often able to judge the wind with remarkable accuracy, the best that a beginner can expect to do is to learn and memorise the known effect of certain defined wind forces, and make a reasonable guess at the prevailing wind's strength and direction. The accuracy of the guess will largely depend on practice and his ability to interpret the evidence provided by the flags and other aids at his disposal. Fortunately, there are several aids, natural and artificial, to provide this evidence, and a beginner can soon learn to be reasonably successful. Wind tables and wind calculators (figure 43) are available, sometimes embodied in score-books, and are useful guides.

The easiest winds to estimate are those which blow across wide open spaces, unhindered by hills, undulations, or obstacles of any sort. They are usually fairly regular in force and direction.

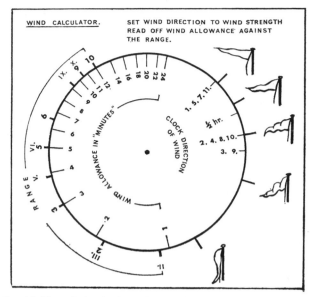

Fig. 43. The wind calculator shown above was designed by Rear-Admiral F. E. P. Hutton C.B., who very kindly permitted its inclusion in this book.

Description The calculator consists of a revolving disc pivoted on the square part which could be the inside cover of a score-book. The flags represent wind strengths of 4, 8, 12, 16 and 20 m.p.h., usually called 'Gentle', 'Moderate', 'Fresh', 'Strong' and 'Very Strong' respectively. The calculator is suitable for either the .303 in. Mark 7 cartridge (using the range marks shown in arabic figures, e.g. '9') or for the 7.62 mm NATO cartridge (using the range marks shown in roman figures, e.g. 'IX'). The calculated wind allowance will be in minutes of angle.

Method of use Set Wind direction to wind strength. Read off wind allowance against range.

The diagram shows the setting for a 'Fresh' wind blowing from 2 o'clock. The wind allowance required at any range can readily be seen e.g. 12 minutes at 1,000 yards (.303 in.), 5 minutes at 600 yards (7.62 mm). If desired a number of possible wind strengths and directions can be tried in order to get an idea of the likely maximum and minimum, and hence a good 'mean wind' to commence with. By setting the calculator to the mean wind allowance found at one particular range, the required allowance for the same wind at other ranges can be read off.

Though often windier in character, rifle ranges situated near the coast and open to the winds blowing from the sea generally present fewer problems than inland ranges situated in hilly and wooded country. The most difficult winds to assess are those which continually change direction, visual evidence generally being much less obvious.

WIND FLAGS. On well equipped rifle ranges, flags or streamers are placed at intervals between the firing-point and the targets to indicate the strength and direction of the wind. They are the best guides for winds blowing at between three and twenty miles per hour. Unless the flags are very light they are unlikely to become animated by wind blowing below three miles per hour. Light flags, however, are of little use in very strong winds and it is therefore important that the wind flags should conform to certain standards. Those in use on the Bisley ranges are suitable in size, shape, and weight—weight being a particularly important factor. The material now used is a form of nylon, which is more sensitive than normal flag bunting and has the advantage of drying more quickly when wet. At Bisley the Stickledown Range flags are fifteen feet long, six feet deep at the hoist, and about twelves inches deep at the fly. For the shorter distances on the Century Range they are two-thirds this size.

The height at which the flags are flown is also important. They should fly as nearly as possible to the trajectory in order to register the wind currents which are actually affecting the bullets. Obviously, the flags must be positioned so as to avoid being struck by bullets. On ranges which are partly sheltered or affected by abnormal wind currents, some modifications to normal flag disposition may have to be made. The important thing is that they show the wind which is likely to affect the bullets.

WIND FORCES. In target shooting, wind is generally considered in five forces: 'gentle' (four miles per hour), 'moderate' (eight miles per hour), 'fresh' (twelves miles per hour), 'strong' (sixteen miles per hour) and 'very strong' (twenty miles per hour). Wind allowances shown on wind calculators—already referred to— are based on these forces. Some of the visual effects which may be expected from various wind forces are given in figure 44.

MIRAGE. In hot weather, heated air rising from the ground produces the visual effect known as mirage. It is particularly apparent when the ground is moist and the sun hot and bright, and it reveals the behaviour of the air movement in a very definite manner. Although sometimes visible to the naked eye, the movements of mirage can best be observed with the aid of a telescope mounted on a suitable stand.

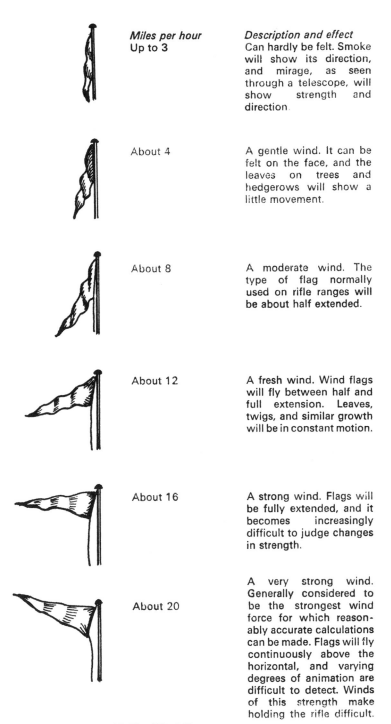

Miles per hour	*Description and effect*
Up to 3	Can hardly be felt. Smoke will show its direction, and mirage, as seen through a telescope, will show strength and direction.
About 4	A gentle wind. It can be felt on the face, and the leaves on trees and hedgerows will show a little movement.
About 8	A moderate wind. The type of flag normally used on rifle ranges will be about half extended.
About 12	A fresh wind. Wind flags will fly between half and full extension. Leaves, twigs, and similar growth will be in constant motion.
About 16	A strong wind. Flags will be fully extended, and it becomes increasingly difficult to judge changes in strength.
About 20	A very strong wind. Generally considered to be the strongest wind force for which reasonably accurate calculations can be made. Flags will fly continuously above the horizontal, and varying degrees of animation are difficult to detect. Winds of this strength make holding the rifle difficult.

Fig. 44. The Wind Flag.

When not animated laterally by moving air currents, mirage looks rather like boiling water and in this state is described as 'boiling'. The lightest of breezes will cause the mirage to move and indicate its direction. It presents a shimmering or wavy appearance similar to running water.

In very hot countries mirage is nearly always present. In more temperate climates it is less frequent but can still be regarded as a valuable aid to wind judgement. When passing clouds obscure the sun for short periods the visibility of mirage becomes intermittent, and in these circumstances its value as a wind guide diminishes and it is better to rely on the flags.

Mirage is of maximum value in gentle winds which cause very little movement of flags. In these conditions it can be seen running or changing direction from side to side, the smallest air movements which cannot be detected by any other means being clearly revealed.

ADDITIONAL AIMS TO WIND JUDGING. Anything which is easily disturbed by wind can be a useful aid in assessing wind strengths, especially on rifle ranges ill-equipped with wind flags or streamers. Leaves, pieces of paper, long grass etc., can convey to an intelligent observer the direction of the wind and often give some indication of its strength.

In the days of black-powder cartridges, the smoke from rifle barrels was keenly watched. On dull days, the light smoke which comes from the modern cordite or N.C. loaded cartridge can also be helpful. In this respect, the rifle of the up-wind neighbour on the firing-point is often worth watching. When cordite smoke is visible, it is of much greater value than the sand often seen flying on the stop-butts as the bullets strike, the latter being of very doubtful value as a guide to wind behaviour.

PRELIMINARY OBSERVATIONS. A marksman need only be concerned with the wind currents that actually affect his bullets. On arriving on a range his first consideration should be:
1. The available aids which will give him true information on the force and direction of the prevailing wind.
2. Whether there are any physical abnormalities or obstacles on or near the range which will affect the wind in such a manner that their effect on the wind will not be shown by the available flags.
   A knowledge of the local conditions of a range is generally helpful.
3. The strength and direction of the wind, the frequency of wind changes and whether they appear to follow any particular pattern.

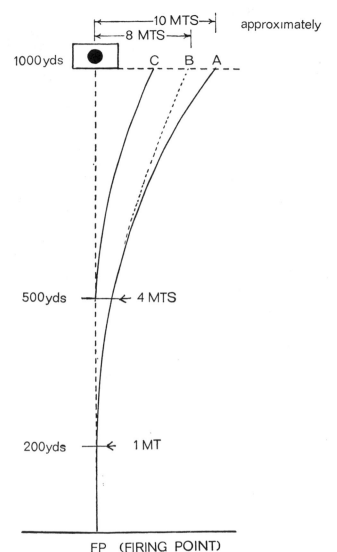

Fig. 45. Wind effects.

FP—Target Line of sight.
FP—A   Approximate course of bullet when subjected to a uniform wind from firing-point to target.
FP—B   Approximate course of bullet when subjected to wind for the first 500 yards of its course and no wind blowing over the last 500 yards.
FP—C   Approximate course of bullet when the first 500 yards is completely sheltered and bullet is subjected to wind for last 500 yards only.

THE FLAGS TO WATCH. On large rifle ranges where there are usually several wind flags it is obvious that one cannot watch them all. The best plan is to concentrate on one flag, giving an occasional glance at others—although it is sometimes preferable to select one particular flag for wind strength and another for direction. Selected flags should be up-wind and registering the wind which will affect the bullet, the directional flag should be blowing straight towards the firer. Only when up-wind flags are not available should down-wind flags be used, as they are showing wind that has passed.

It is not always understood why flags nearer the firer than the target are of greater importance as wind aids, some people inclining to the view that as the bullet's velocity drops so its susceptibility to the effect of wind increases. The explanation is that once a bullet is deflected from its course by wind it does not recover its initial direction, even if no wind affects the latter part of its flight. Consequently, the further a bullet travels after being blown off its course the greater will be the error at the target (figure 45).

If the first part of a bullet's flight is sheltered by trees or something similar, and later part of its flight is exposed to the full force of the wind, it will inevitably be the flags nearer the target which will give the firer some idea of what wind allowance to make. Obviously, however, the evidence of these flags will have to be treated circumspectly and less than the full allowance indicated by them should be made. Good examples of partly sheltered ranges can be seen at Bisley (plate 54).

DIRECTIONAL ASSESSMENT. Determination of direction is one of the more difficult aspects of wind judging. Changes in direction are often very quick, and—unless one is fortunate in having a flag blowing almost straight towards one—it is frequently impossible to detect a directional change. In these circumstances, especially if the wind is strong, even experienced marksmen get into difficulties.

A simple method of describing the direction from which wind is blowing is employed in target shooting. The firer considers himself to be in the centre of a clock-face with the target representing twelve o'clock, the numerals around the clock-face denoting the direction of the wind. Thus, a wind blowing at right-angles to the line of fire is either a three-o'clock or a nine o'clock wind. A head wind blows from twelve o'clock and a following wind from six o'clock (figure 46).

The maximum bullet deflection results from direct cross-

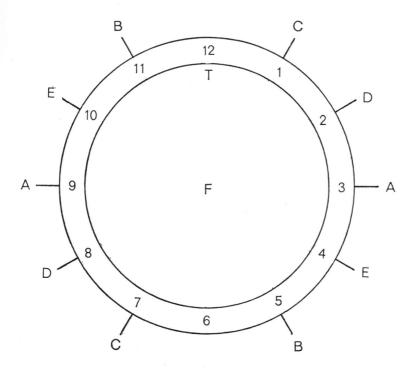

T=TARGET   F= FIRER

WINDS A to A   =   MAXIMUM DEFLECTION

  "   B to B ⎱ _ 1
  "   C to C ⎰ = —   "   "
                        2

  "   D to D ⎱ _ 7
  "   E to E ⎰ = —   "   "
                        8

Fig. 46. Clock-face directional assessment. While wind changes D to A to E, and vice-versa, have relatively little effect, those from B to C and C to B are extremely important.

winds, i.e. three or nine o'clock winds, Winds from one, five, seven and eleven o'clock cause half the amount of deflection of a direct cross-wind (figure 46). These assessments are near enough for all practical target shooting purposes, and provide a sound basis for wind judging. Following and head winds are usually known as 'zero' winds as they need no deflection allowance. When changing direction from side to side they are called 'fishtailing' winds.

How to Allow for Wind. There are two methods of allowing for wind:

1. Aiming off into the wind the requisite distance from the centre of the target. This is compulsory for Service rifle shooting.
2. Making the necessary allowance on the backsight. This enables the line of sight, or aim, to be directed at the target while the rifle barrel points to the required angle.

Two methods of determining wind allowance are:

1. By estimating the allowance for each individual shot.
2. By acting on the preceding shots on a plus or minus basis.

The first method gives a marksman much more practice in forming mental pictures of the wind flags or mirage for any particular force or direction of wind. As he becomes more proficient in wind judging he will probably get the best results from a combination of both methods. The following gives an outline of what the authors consider the best procedure to follow:

1. Look at the chosen flag. Note the angle at which it is flying and the degree of animation, and decide on the wind force. The novice will find a wind calculator with sketches of flags depicting various wind forces of considerable value (figure 43).
2. Mentally convert the assessment into minutes of angle. With a little experience, wind assessments will automatically be made in this manner. This is most necessary as calculations must be made quickly.
3. Make the required sight adjustment and get the shot away as quickly as possible. Good wind judging is often completely ruined by slow shooting, the wind may have changed by the time the bullet is in the air.
4. The beginner is advised not to 'fiddle' with wind corrections. In his early shooting career he will be insufficiently

experienced to read very small changes but when he is sure that a change has occured the chances are that it is a fairly definite one and he can make a bold correction with reasonable confidence. When in doubt he should endeavour to ascertain a 'mean' wind somewhere between the maximum and minimum strengths indicated by the flags and other aids. Relatively small changes above and below the mean wind will probably be all that is required to give him a reasonable shoot. However, like all other matters connected with wind judging, this is more easily said than done.

5. In strong gusty winds, confirmation that an extra strong gust has occured can often be obtained by a quick look at the targets in the immediate vicinity of one's own. If a number of them show similar indications of blown shots, due allowance can be made providing the conditions still appear the same when one is ready to shoot. If the wind seems to have resumed its normal strength, no sight adjustment should be made. It should always be remembered that in gusty conditions the gusts and lulls are generally of short duration, and it is frequently a matter of luck whether or not a firer is caught by one when actually aiming. In these conditions, the necessity of getting shots away quickly is obvious.

MAKING A SIGHT CORRECTION FOR WIND. A sight correction for wind should only be made when there is a definite change in strength or direction. When one's group appears to be forming away from the centre of the target, the necessary corrections should be made but should not be confused with corrections for wind.

When an unmistakable change in wind strength or direction occurs, it will need at least a one-minute correction at ranges from 300 to 600 yards. Only in very light winds is a smaller change discernible. At 900 and 1,000 yards a minimum discernible change seldom requires less than two minutes correction, except in light and fishtailing winds. With a strong wind blowing across the range it is difficult at long range to estimate changes of less than three to four minutes. It must be borne in mind that what appears to be a two minute change when at 500 yards, may need at least a five minute correction at 1,000 yards. A reasonably accurate rule is to make double the wind allowance at 900 and 1,000 yards that would be required in similar conditions at 500 and 600 yards respectively.

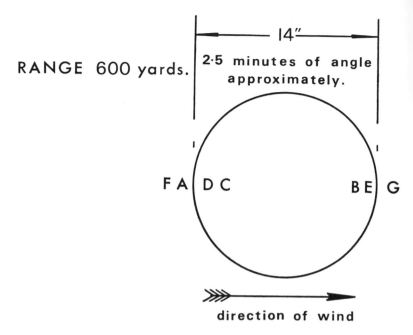

Fig. 47. Making allowance for wind.

AN EXAMPLE OF MAKING ALLOWANCE FOR WIND (figure 47).
1. Assume that a left wind is blowing, appearing to require a five-minute sight correction, and that the sight has been adjusted accordingly.
2. The first shot strikes near the left edge of the bulls-eye (A). Bearing in mind that one's group—without personal error —can be assumed to be within the limits of the bulls-eye, there is no means of knowing whether the shot is the left, right, or centre shot of the ultimate group, or whether the wind has been over estimated. As this is the first sighting shot, the second sighter should be fired before making any alteration (as explained in chapter 7). If the second shot falls in the right half of the bull somewhere near (B), it can be assumed that wind assessment is reasonably accurate and that the two shots represent the probable extremes of the group.
3. If, however, the second shot strikes near (C) and there was no obvious change of wind, the two shots suggest that somewhere near A-C is the group centre and the wind has

been over-estimated. A full allowance should be made from the mean of A and C, i.e. reduce the wind correction by one minute. The firer should now have formed a reasonably good mental picture of a four-minute left wind, which' should help throughout the shoot.

4. Should the third shot go near (D) or (E), it is within the limitations of rifle and cartridge and not necessarily due to an unnoticed wind change. If this shot had been influenced by a small wind change it would probably have gone near (F) or (G). Unless reasonably sure of a wind change, indiscriminate sight alterations should not be made. They only lead to confusion and loss of the mental picture of how one's group is forming. If this picture is lost, so is the basis of all future sight corrections during the shoot. The picture of the group should not only be a mental one. Each shot should be carefully plotted in the score-book (see chapter 12). If this has been done correctly, the group centre of the first three shots and the 'mean' wind should now have been reasonably well determined, enabling the firer to continue shooting with confidence.

WIND JUDGING BY MIRAGE. The ability to read wind by mirage can only be acquired by experience. There is no yardstick, and no tables or calculators illustrating degrees of wind strength and direction can be applied. To the experienced marksman, mirage is the truest guide as it conveys to him an ever-moving picture of the wind through which the bullets travel.

A telescope used for reading mirage should be of at least twenty magnifications and, as it must be kept steady, it should be mounted on a rigid stand. This should be positioned so that the firer, in a normal, comfortable firing position, can look through the telescope with a minimum of head movement.

The telescope should show the mirage indicating the wind through which the bullets will travel, and should be focused at about one-third the distance from the firing-point to the target. The target and spotting disc should still be sufficiently visible.

Mirage is particularly useful in 'fishtailing' winds as it immediately records changes of light air movements. Quick shooting is again desirable, for obvious reasons.

It sometimes happens that mirage is seen running in the opposite direction to wind-flag movement, in which case it is generally safer to rely on mirage, this being nearer to the actual flight of the bullet.

When air movements are in the same general direction as the

line of sight, i.e. from six or twelve o'clock, the mirage 'boil' becomes very animated in appearance. Wind blowing at an angle to the line of sight is clearly visible by fast-running mirage.

In wind moving at more than seven to eight miles per hour, mirage loses its value as a guide. Changes of strength become difficult to assess and it is better to rely on the flags. When mirage becomes invisible, it can sometimes be brought into view again by slowly opening the eye which is not looking through the telescope. When doing this, the concentration of the 'telescope eye' must not be relaxed.

It is important to remember that up to 600 yards the bullet does not rise much above the firer's line of sight to the top of the target (figure 25, chapter 6), so that mirage which is showing the wind actually affecting the bullet can easily be brought into view. Hence, mirage may not be a very reliable guide at long ranges and frequently a compromise between wind-flags and mirage has to be made.

Final Words of Advice.

1. At all times be honest. Do not blame the wind for what are more likely to be personal errors.

2. Do not pay too much attention to the comments of others who have just fired. Their rifle zeros may be incorrect, their wind judgment may be faulty, and all allowances they have made may be quite different from those required when it is your turn to shoot. If you want advice, ask only those marksmen you know can be relied on and use the information obtained only to confirm your own impressions.

3. Enter every sight alteration in the score-book. Some marksmen sketch a small wind-flag in their book showing the angle at which the wind is blowing at the commencement of a shoot, followed by sketches showing any changes that take place during the shoot. This can be a useful reference as the shoot progresses. Others make a note of the wind allowance required for each shot to bring it to the vertical centre-line. Anything which helps to complete the score-book picture should be done.

SHOOTING IN THE RAIN. Shooting in rain is not only unpleasant, it often presents a problem to which there is no easy solution. In addition to its effect on the firer in terms of discomfort, misted-up spectacles or lenses, rain-sodden score-books and register tickets, slippery rifle woodwork and so on, there is the mechanical effect on rifle and cartridge which can also help to destroy a marksman's hope of success. The shooter who can resolve these problems and make scores in rain comparable to those he would normally expect to make in fine weather can sometimes turn unpleasant shooting conditions to his advantage.

Water on a cartridge case or in a rifle chamber acts like a lubricant in much the same way as oil. When it is present a cartridge case cannot grip the inner surface of the chamber, resulting in greatly increased pressure on the face of the bolt-head. This inevitably has some effect on the vibratory behaviour of the barrel and action, and influences the departure of the bullet.

In the case of rifles with Lee-Enfield type actions such as the No. 4 rifle, the locking lugs are about four inches behind the bolt face. In rifles with forward locking actions such as the Mausers, the distance is only about three-quarters of an inch. With the former, extra pressure on the bolt face, coupled with the inevitable 'give' or spring in the body (receiver), is likely to affect barrel vibrations to a much greater extent than on Mauser and similar type actions. It can increase the angle of projection of a No. 4 Rifle by as much as four to five minutes, though this varies between rifles. The majority of forward locking actions are relatively unaffected by moisture in the chamber, at any rate as far as bullet behaviour is concerned.

Quite apart from irregular performance caused by shooting with wet ammunition, there is a strong likelihood of damaging the rifle. In the normal way, with dry cartridges, a high proportion of the chamber pressure is absorbed through friction by the chamber itself. When wet, the whole of the chamber pressure is transmitted direct to the recoil lugs on the bolt. In Lee-Enfield type rifles, one of these is in the form of a rib running most of the length of the bolt. This is unlikely to fracture as the Lee-Enfield type of action is extremely strong, but the small lug on the opposite side of the bolt is much more fragile. There have been numerous instances of this lug cracking or breaking off due to shooting with wet cartridges or water in the chamber. If this happens, there is little risk to the firer but the accuracy of the rifle is seriously affected and a new bolt will be required. In the case of the P.'14 rifle, there have been instances of one and sometimes both of the recoil lugs breaking off as a result of firing with wet ammunition. With the 7.62 mm cartridge, which gives appreciably higher chamber pressure than the .303 in. round, the risk of damage is likely to be greater. It will therefore be appreciated that firing 'wet' is a policy of desperation and should not be resorted to if it is possible to avoid it.

41

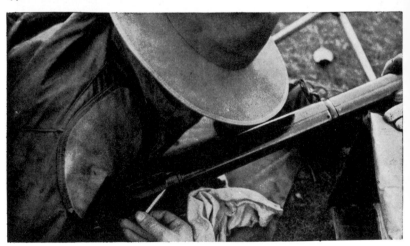

42

Plate 41. One way of keeping a score-book dry while making the necessary entries. The firer has a spare groundsheet wrapped around his shooting case.

Plate 42. Keeping the ammunition dry. Rifle drawn well under the firer and turned on its side while a fresh round is fed into the chamber. Note the wash-leather ready to hand.

The following methods are recommended for keeping one's ammunition and rifle action dry:

1. Procure a waterproof case in which ammunition and score-book etc. can be kept away from driving rain.
2. Keep a chamois leather or small towel in the shooting case for wiping the action before opening the bolt—a chamois leather being preferable.
3. A ground-sheet is useful to cover the gap between case and rifle (plate 41), though it tends to collect water which may run-off when re-loading and cause trouble.
4. When loading, withdraw the rifle as much as possible under the body, turn it on its side in the opposite direction to driving rain (plate 56), wipe off all water from the action before opening the bolt, then quickly transfer a round from case to rifle chamber and immediately close the bolt.
5. An alternative and probably better method is to keep the cartridges in an inside pocket of one's shooting coat or in a waterproof bag tucked inside the coat. With the rifle drawn well under the body, cartridge and rifle chamber are not so vulnerable to rain during the operation of loading. A piece of towel should be kept in or near the ammunition pocket to dry the hand before it touches the cartridge.
6. Some marksmen eject the empty cases and reload immediately after firing, hoping that the hot chamber will dry the round. The authors prefer to keep the bolt closed and to reload just before shooting, obviating the danger of a round over-heating due to long delay in a hot chamber. The latter method is unquestionably the safer.
7. A groundsheet is not a good thing to lie on in heavy rain. It quickly collects water and adds to the discomfort and difficulty of wet weather shooting.

SPECTACLES AND LENSES. Marksmen who have to wear spectacles are at a distinct disadvantage in rain as it is extremely difficult to keep the lenses clear of water. A broad-brimmed hat tied under the chin is of considerable help, and care should be taken not to touch the glasses with the hands. If the lenses get so wet as seriously to affect aiming, the best solution is to wipe the glasses with a chamois leather and replace them—under the hat brim— as quickly as possible.

The problem is less acute if a lens in the eyepiece can be used instead of spectacles, though eyepiece lenses can be affected by

43

Plate 43. Prismatic spotting telescope with 60 mm object lens and magnifying power of 20X. This type of telescope is largely used for competition shooting and is mounted on a bipod type stand which enables the firer to get close enough to look through the telescope without undue movement of head and shoulders, and obviates the risk of touching the stand with his arm.

rain. A rubber or plastic eyecup over the eyepiece is permitted and gives useful protection. In rainy weather, the long-sighted marksman is at the greatest disadvantage as, though he may be able to aim adequately with a lens in his eyepiece, he may be unable to see his score-book. But this must be regarded as of relatively minor importance in the circumstances.

THE TELESCOPE. Another wet weather problem concerns the telescope, particularly the draw-tube type, Unless protected, it can soon become useless in driving rain, the lenses becoming completely fogged up. A plastic cover is an effective safeguard.

Useful emergency protection can be obtained from a piece of thin cardboard such as a small-bore target, or even a newspaper wrapped round the tube and protruding at the front end to protect the object lens. Do not wait until the rain commences before protecting the telescope.

A wet telescope should be dried immediately after use, the lenses being carefully wiped with a soft, clean cloth. The draw-tube type may have to be completely dismantled if the inner lenses fog up due to condensation. On no account should this type of telescope be closed while it is wet.

AFTER-CARE. A rifle needs special attention after wet weather shooting. The woodwork should immediately be wiped and oiled with linseed oil. It should not be dried out in direct hot sunshine or by artificial heat. If allowed to dry naturally, the woodwork is far less liable to shrink or warp. A rifle should never be laid on wet ground, especially in strong sunshine. In such conditions, one side of the stock fore-end may swell and the other side shrink, causing a complete upset of the stocking-up bearings.

All the metal parts of the rifle should be cleaned and wiped with an oily cloth as a safeguard against rust. If the rifle is to be used again the same day, care must be taken against leaving oil in the bolt-way, for reasons already explained. Modern 'de-watering' oils are available in spray packs and they are extremely useful for dealing with wet firearms.

11

SHOOTING EQUIPMENT

THE CHOICE OF SHOOTING EQUIPMENT. In most sporting pastimes there is an assortment of gadgets, many of which are designed to capture the imagination of the enthusiast. Often, the pleasure and anticipation of purchase outweighs their usefulness.

In target shooting, most available gadgets have a sound practical application and help to produce slightly better results with less individual effort from the user. Inevitably, there are a number of 'gimmicks' that are of little value and which one can well do without. The object of this chapter is to advise on what are considered to be essential items of target shooting equipment.

THE RIFLE. The purchaser is strongly recommended to buy his target rifle from one of the small number of firearms dealers who specialise in this particular branch of the trade, and who are expert in the skilled adjustment of rifles for competitive shooting. In this respect, an important consideration is that these specialist firms can provide the after-sales service necessary in maintaining the highest standard of rifle accuracy. A Service calibre target rifle should be 'tuned up' periodically and the most convenient time for this, for both shooter and armourer, is during the winter months. An armourer who is himself a practising marksman is more likely to understand a shooter's problems and provide the answers than one who is merely a retailer and has little interest beyond a purely financial one. This should not be overlooked when buying a target rifle.

Any temptation to buy a cheap rifle simply because it is cheap should be resisted. A person experienced in weapons and familiar with the many points to be considered may be fortunate in purchasing an inexpensive rifle in good order, but a novice may acquire one that gives him consistently bad results and adversely affects his enthusiasm for shooting; he may even feel inclined to give it up for some other form of sporting pastime.

Additionally, a cheap defective rifle will inevitably cost more in the long run than a really good guaranteed weapon.

The defects most likely to be found will be a worn out or badly pitted barrel, concealed splits, warping and other woodwork faults, worn action mechanism and aperture sight, and the stocking-up will almost certainly need attention. Any of the above defects can render a rifle quite useless for accurate shooting. In competitive shooting, apart from disappointment, a considerable amount of money can be wasted in entry fees and ammunition.

As a marksman becomes established, he will probably feel the need for more than one rifle. Indications are that if he wishes to excel, or even to hold his own, at all competition distances from 200 to 1,000 yards he will require at least two rifles, one for ranges up to 600 yards and another for the longer distances. As a general principle, the Mauser (forward locking action) type will probably give the best results at short ranges and the converted No. 4, rifle is likely to be superior at long ranges (chapter 3).

Quite apart from other considerations, it is prudent to have a second string to one's bow. There is always the chance of something unexpectedly going wrong and when this happens at an important shoot or prize meeting, the chance of success is jeopardised.

The wide variety of available 7.62 mm target rifles makes choice and recommendation difficult and a visit to a specialist gunsmith is advisable. Here, the respective purchaser can handle the various makes of rifle and receive personal advice on which seem the most suitable for his particular requirements. Alternatively, illustrated detailed catalogues are generally available. In some clubs there may be opportunities of trying out different types of rifles belonging to club members.

Rifles fall naturally into two types; those with target-style stocks with broad fore-ends, cheek-pieces and high butt combs etc., and those with stocks built more on Service rifle lines. The latter have narrower fore-ends, handguards and simple butts without cheek-pieces but with fairly high butt combs and pistol grips (chapter 3). In advising on choice, one can only emphasise that comfort is essential and the rifle which 'fits' its firer is likely to be the more successful. The 'Custom' or hand finished rifle is recommended as the best investment in the long run.

The marksman who has No. 4 or P. '14 Rifles suitable for conversion would do well to have one of these modified to fire the 7.62 mm cartridge. He can subsequently add to his armoury when he has had an opportunity of assessing the other types of target rifles. The newcomer to the sport is advised to go initially for a forward locking (Mauser) type of rifle as he will probably do most of his shooting at short ranges (200 to 600 yards). He can later acquire a Lee-Enfield actioned rifle for long range shooting.

Interchangeable foresights are invariably fitted to modern target rifles (chapter 10), and an additional refinement worth consideration is an adjustable or 'Match' trigger.

THE GUN BARRELS PROOF ACT AND THE FIREARMS ACT. Advice on the purchase of firearms would be incomplete without mention of the Proof and Firearms Acts and their implications regarding target rifles in the United Kingdom.

Under the Gun Barrels Proof Act 1868, all firearms, rifled or otherwise, must be submitted to either the London or the Birmingham Proof House before they can be sold. Here, the barrels are subjected to expert examination for flaws or other defects. If satisfactory, the barrels are tested by firing a specially loaded oiled Proof round; the Proof charge being substantially heavier than the normal load. This is followed by another careful examination and, if the firearm passes this satisfactorily, it is

Fig. 48. Sale permit mark.

marked with the appropriate Proof mark. Certain other information, such as length of chamber and mean pressure, is also stamped on the barrel. The proof of military weapons, as carried out at Royal Ordance Factories, is a similar routine but generally includes the firing of one oiled and one dry proof round. The purpose of the oiled round is to cause the maximum amount of pressure to be exerted on the breech face instead of being largely absorbed by the barrel chamber walls, as is the case when the dry round is fired. Military proof marks are only acceptable for private sale purposes when weapons additionally bear the 'Sale Permit' mark. This consists of two broad arrows with their points touching, surmounted by the letter 'S' (figure 48).

No firearm should be bought until the purchaser is satisfied that the proof marks are in order as required by law. Expert advice should be sought when any doubt exists.

Of equal importance is compliance with the Firearms Act. No person under 17 years of age may acquire a rifled firearm of any description, except in special circumstances when a parent or guardian undertakes full responsibility for the supervision and instruction of the user of such a weapon. In this event, two Firearm Certificates may be issued, one to each party. The firearm may be entered on both certificates with a proviso in the case of the junior that it may only be used under the supervision of the senior person until the former attains the age of 17 years. The term 'acquire' means to buy, hire, borrow, or receive as a gift, and in each case the procedure is the same.

In the normal way, the potential purchaser of a firearm should make application for a Firearm Certificate to the Police, who will supply him with a form for completion which must be handed in at the local Police Station. Enquiries will be made to ensure that the applicant is a suitable person to own firearms. The Police must also be satisfied that the applicant has facilities for safe storage and that the weapons are required for a genuine purpose such as target shooting on approved ranges and under the auspices of an approved rifle or pistol club.

When the Certificate is granted, it should be taken to the vendor of the required weapon, or weapons, and he will make the necessary entry in Table 1. The latter is the appropriate space for recording details of all acquisitions of firearms. The obligation is then on the vendor to notify the Police within 48 hours of the transaction and provide details of the firearm supplied. Home Office Firearms Form 11 is used for this purpose.

It is unnecessary when applying for authority to acquire a firearm to provide details of the serial number and description of the weapon it is intended to buy. Very often these details are not available until the purchase is actually made. All that is legally required on application is the quantity and type of firearm and calibre, e.g. one 7.62 mm target rifle. Full details are provided by the vendor when the transaction actually takes place.

The initial grant of a Firearm Certificate may authorise the holder to acquire one or more weapons. If he wishes to acquire more at a later date, or dispose of his original purchase and possibly obtain a different make, application must be made to the Police for a variation of his certificate. A form of application for variations and renewals will be provided by the Police.

Ammunition is dealt with in a similar manner. Authority is given for the certificate holder to have in his possession at any one time, or to purchase or acquire at any one time, limited quantities of the specified ammunition.

A Firearm Certificate must be renewed every three years. In certain circumstances, particularly in the case of members of small-bore rifle clubs, authority to acquire ammunition may not be granted, on the assumption that the certificate holder can purchase his requirements at his club for immediate use on the range.

On no account should firearms be purchased or acquired other than from a registered firearms dealer, or from the holder of a valid Firearm Certificate on which the weapon concerned is entered.

APERTURE SIGHTS AND EYEPIECES. Aperture sights have been dealt with in chapter 7 and, as the variety is somewhat limited, the beginner can safely be left to make his own choice. Any of the recognised makes will give good service and satisfy normal requirements. When purchasing, the sight should be critically examined in both vertical and lateral movements to ensure that there is no backlash (chapter 7). To check this point, move the adjusting knobs a certain number of clicks in one direction and then move them back the same number of clicks; the vernier scales should be in eactly the same position as they were before they were moved.

There is also a limited choice of eyepieces. One of the variable type—either six-hole or iris—is recommended as it gives a selection of aperture size. Iris eyepieces (figure 40, chapter 10) have an advantage in that the aperture cannot get out of centre. They can, however, be accidentally altered and care should be taken to ensure that the setting is correct. This also applies to six-hole eyepieces which can get out of centre and completely ruin a shoot, as many marksmen have found to their cost. The cup or tubular type is preferable to the flat variety as it is less likely to reflect light from behind. It can also be used to house a filter if required and can be fitted with a rubber or plastic cup or shade. For those who have to use an optical lens to correct their eyesight, the Steward lensholder attachment (figure 49) is recommended.

TELESCOPES AND STANDS. The modern telescope has a large object lens, approximately 60 mm in diameter, and is usually prismatic with screw adjustable focus. The older types with two or more draws are less advantageous as they often fog up badly in wet weather. Their length makes them more difficult to manipulate on crowded firing-points.

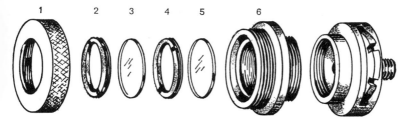

Fig. 49. The Steward lens-holder. The Steward lens-holder is designed to take an optical lens and a coloured filter. It fits most conventional 6-hole and iris eyepieces. Parts 1 to 6 comprise the lens-holder, optical lens, filter, and securing rings.

Prismatic telescopes, as used in target shooting, are only about sixteen ins. in length. Some have angled eyepieces enabling the firer to take a quick look at the mirage or target without disturbing his firing position. Others, with straight eyepieces, are somewhat less expensive. The popular magnification for normal range work is 20X, giving the user a good field of view, ample visibility when the light is poor, and a satisfactory picture of everything a marksman wants to see.

Probably the best mount for a prismatic telescope is one of the bipod type (plate 43), which enable the telescope to be positioned close to the firer's eye with little risk of his arm touching the stand. Some telescopes are supplied with folding tripods which can generally be arranged to avoid being touched by the arm. In competition shooting, range officers quite rightly watch for any suggestion of a competitor resting his arm on his telescope stand, and the rule covering this point is strictly enforced.

SHOOTING CLOTHING. Competitive shooting does not stop for bad weather and there is always the possibility of having to shoot in rain. A waterproof shooting coat is therefore an essential item of target shooting equipment. The alternative may be oilskins or the like—which do not have the 'feel' of what is normally worn. Unfamiliar clothing, coupled with the inevitable discomfort of shooting in the rain can certainly have an adverse effect on scores. Broadly speaking, therefore, it is important to be able to shoot in much the same outfit wet or fine, simply adding a pair of waterproof over-trousers when it is wet. The only disadvantage is that a waterproof coat can become a little oppressive in very hot weather. This, however, is a relatively small point as the actual shooting calls for little physical exertion. The best solution is, of course, to have two coats as nearly identical as possible, one waterproofed and the other made of unproofed light cotton or linen material. But the shooter of limited means is advised to go for the waterproof coat until he can afford the luxury of both.

SHOOTING COATS. Most coats made for target shooting have elbow, shoulder and sling pads attached in their correct positions, and there are coats available for either left or right-handed shooters. When purchasing a coat for shooting with the Target Rifle, it is important to ensure that it conforms with the regulations laid down by one's National Rifle Association (see chapter 17 for British N.R.A. regulations). For World Championship events one must conform to the rules of the International Shooting Union.

HATS. Broad-brimmed hats help to shelter the firer and back-sight from sun and rain and, if desired, the brim can be tied down to form a shield for the non-aiming eye. The best type of shooting hat is probably the felt 'bush hat' similar to that worn by the Australian armed forces. Official broad-brimmed hats are usually issued to members of teams representing their countries on international tours. Although the basic purpose is to ensure that the teams are equipped with practical shooting-hats, they add a certain glamour to the wearers, especially in international matches with each team wearing distinctive coloured hat bands.

GLOVES. A shooting glove is frequently in evidence, worn on the hand supporting the rifle. Its purpose is to prevent the hand from slipping on the rifle fore-end and protect the back of the hand from chafing by the sling. Padded and gauntlet type gloves which are 'stiffened' are not permitted under British N.R.A. rules and the most popular type is a light glove or mitt which allow the fingers to protrude. An old leather glove with the finger ends cut off is suitable and special gloves of this nature are commercially available. Under International Shooting Union rules, the gloves must not extend more than 5 cms (about 2 ins.) above the wrist, and must not be thicker than 5 mms (about 1/5th in.).

ELBOW PADS. Marksmen who do not possess or do not like padded shooting coats usually wear elbow pads for protection and these satisfactorily meet limited requirements. There are several varieties of strap-on elbow pads and those made of rubber—i.e. crepe with sponge lining—are particularly recommended. Under N.R.A. rules they may not be worn over a padded coat if the thickness exceeds ½-in. They may be worn with uniform when the wearing of it is obligatory.

SCORE BOOK. A score book is an essential item of a target rifle marksman's equipment and its correct use plays an important part in his early training. There are several kinds of available score books from which to choose, according to price and personal appeal. One of the better types is that embodying the loose-leaf system in which a whole page is devoted to one range diagram. This arrangement enables the book to be adapted to personal requirements; in wet weather only those diagram sheets essential for the shoot need be taken on to the range. Diagrams outlined for 15-round shoots are a definite requirement.

USE OF THE SCORE BOOK. To be of real value, a score book should be regarded as of much greater significance than a mere record of scores. Reference to a carefully kept score book should give a lead to the cause of troubles that have been experienced during a shoot, and prevent errors and miscalculations from being repeated.

A common fault is to plot shots on the diagrams closer to the centre than they really are. While this makes the score book look better when showing it to friends, the owner of the book is only deceiving and misleading himself. To be of any value all score book entries must be strictly honest and accurate. Figures 50 and 51 show the right and wrong way to complete a score book diagram.

The following are a few simple rules for keeping a score book:

1. Use a sharp pencil but not an indelible pencil, which would certainly give trouble in wet weather.
2. Plot on the diagram the exact position of each shot with a small neat number corresponding to the order in which the shot is fired. Sighting shots are usually marked 'A' and 'B' and subsequent shots to count for score are numbered from 1 to the last shot of the series (figure 50).
3. The vernier scale sight reading for elevation should be recorded in the appropriate space and any subsequent elevation changes should be similarly recorded, i.e. vernier readings.
4. Wind allowance, right or left, should be recorded for each shot.

5. Enter the date, the time, the range on which the shoot takes place, the ammunition used (make and date of ammunition manufacture), very brief description of the weather, and the serial number of the rifle. The latter item is particularly important when the firer owns more than one rifle.

6. Do not use what is known as the 'spider's legs' method of recording a shoot (figure 51). This is difficult to follow—and if you have to show your score-book to your gunsmith for any reason connected with rifle trouble which you want him to correct, you may present him with another problem he will not appreciate.

7. Most score books have space for plotting an elevation graph. This is the corrected vertical position of each shot fired; all shots being plotted as if they were fired with the same elevation, corrections being made for any sight elevation adjustments during the shoot. The method of doing this is shown at figure 50.

CLEANING REQUISITES. The main requirement for cleaning a rifle is a cleaning-rod, usually made of steel. Most modern rods have a plastic covering which prevents damage to the rifling. Of necessity, such rods are less strong than plain steel ones and must therefore not be forced into the barrel to an extent likely to bend them unduly and cause them to snap. Most modern cleaning-rods have ball-bearing handles made either of wood or moulded plastic. These enable the rod to rotate with the rifling, thus reducing the tendency for screwed-on implements to un-screw themselves during the process of cleaning. For those who require a rod that can be packed into a comparatively small space, jointed rods are available. These must be handled with care as they are very easily broken.

Brass Detachable Jag   Celluloid Covered Rod   Wood Rod Guide   Rod Stop   Ball-bearing Handle

Fig. 52. Cleaning rod and accessories.

Nearly all the cleaning-rods used in the United Kingdom and throughout the Commonwealth are of British make and have common threads. Rod fittings are therefore interchangeable. The minimum requirements in rod fittings are a brass jag, bristle or nylon brush, and a wool mop. A phosphor-bronze brush is

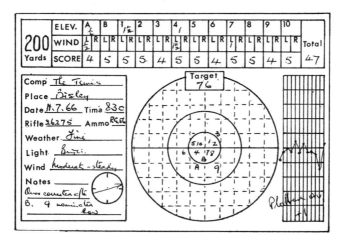

Fig. 50. Correctly completed score-book diagram. Each shot is marked by a neat figure, all elevation and wind sale readings entered and useful information regarding rifle, ammunition, weather, etc. recorded. The elevation graph has been plotted as though all shots were fired with a sight reading of +1, the two sighters and first three shots to count being corrected appropriately.

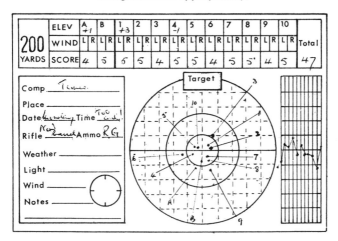

Fig. 51. Incorrectly completed score-book diagram. 'Spider's legs' difficult to follow. Scanty and practically useless information on rifle and ammunition, none on weather conditions or target number. Elevation readings recorded in 'clicks', wind readings omitted altogether. Elevation graph not corrected, and therefore quite valueless and misleading, giving the impression that the shoot was worse than it really was.

useful, though its application should be limited. Other useful items are a rod-guide and rod-stop (figure 52).

The proper material for cleaning a rifle barrel is flannelette. This is sold in rolls, marked with red lines at two-inch intervals, or in packets cut to the correct size, i e. 4 x 2 ins. This size, when correctly wrapped on a jag (Plates 44 to 48 chapter 13), fits the bore of a .303 in. or 7.62 mm barrel sufficiently tightly to clean the bore throughly without getting stuck. For the initial application of a cleaning oil or paste a slightly smaller patch will probably be necessary. There are a number of proprietory brands of cleaning oils, nitro solvents, preserving oils and greases, and bore polishing compounds, obtainable from gunsmiths who cater for the target shooter. The beginner should consult his gunsmith on this matter and follow his advice.

Shooting Bags, Cases and Rifle Covers. The main purpose of a shooting bag or case is probably one of convenience; that of having all one's minor requirements in one container. If one is late for a detail in competition shooting, and all requirements for the shoot are already in the bag or case, last-minute anxiety and confusion may be averted. It also has a real use on the firing-point, especially in wet weather.

The minimum shooting-bag requirement is a haversack, which can be bought quite cheaply. This will hold a score book, ammunition, score cards, glove, duster, washleather and most other necessitiies on the firing-point. More elaborate bags which include loops for cartridges and separate compartments for other items, are probably well worth the extra outlay. For the more affluent there are excellent leather shooting-cases which embody flaps to protect the score book and other contents from rain, in addition to various interior fittings. Some cases are large enough to hold telescope and stand and even a ground-sheet. Though a desirable item of equipment, a large case takes up a lot of room on the firing-point and can be an annoyance to a neighbouring shooter. An interesting exercise in joinery can be undertaken by those competent to make their own shooting-cases from wood and fibre-glass materials. Some ingenious improvisations have been produced from ammunition boxes.

The beginner is advised to start with a simple haversack. On the ranges he will note what other people are using and will eventually see the type of bag or case he fancies.

A rifle cover is essential for the person who has to travel to and from the ranges by public transport, as the law demands that firearms are suitably covered in such circumstances. But in any event, for all forms of travel and on the range in wet weather, some form of protective covering is necessary, and the most convenient is a carrying case with sling attached. There are many types available and price will probably be the deciding factor in making a choice.

THE SLING. A sling is essential for target rifle shooting. As has already been stated, the two-point sling is in general use, either made of leather or webbing. There are firm devotees of both types. Which to use is a matter of personal choice as they are equally satisfactory.

When wet, webbing is inclined to shrink slightly and to harden. Leather will stretch slightly in early life and, if not cared for and regularly oiled with neatsfoot or castor oil, will become hard and eventually crack. Webbing slings have leather ends for attachment to the rifle. Generally speaking, there is probably a slight preference for the leather sling.

When purchasing a sling it is advisable to examine the buckles for signs of weakness. These are usually made of cast brass and are occasionally defective. If a buckle or sling-end disintegrates during a shoot it can be very disturbing for the firer. Some marksmen dispense with buckles and adjust their slings for length by means of leather laces threaded through holes in the sling. The holes are punched in pairs, sufficient in number for considerable adjustment. This method is recommended, providing the sling is kept to one particular rifle; it cannot easily be transferred to another.

THE SINGLE-POINT SLING. If a single-point sling is preferred, there are two main designs to choose from:
1. The leather loop sling. (plates 28 to 30). This is attached to the upper sling swivel and is adjustable for length by means of a buckle. The loop portion through which the arm is passed may be wider than the remainder—up to the permissible maximum of 2 ins., and may be lined with rubber or other non-slip material. A sliding runner prevents the sling from slipping down the arm and may be augmented with a 'sling keeper' a metal clamp operated by a thumb screw. An ordinary leather sling, adjustable by buckle or lace, can easily be adapted into an improvised single-point sling.
2. The cuff sling—made in two parts and undoubtedly the best type of single-point sling. It consists of a short sling

which is attached to the rifle at the forward swivel, and a cuff which straps round the upper arm. The cuff section hooks on to the sling. While waiting to shoot, the short sling can be unhooked from the cuff and left hanging on the rifle, the cuff remaining on the arm. This type of sling can be purchased made in either webbing or leather.

A minor objection to the single-point sling is that it is practically useless for the sling's original purpose, i.e. carrying the rifle. However, other methods of dealing with this can be easily found.

THE RIFLE REST. Of the minor shooting accessories, one of the more useful is a rifle rest. This is a two-pronged fork with a spiked end to push into the ground. It is usually about eight ins. in length. The fork is shaped to hold the rifle fore-end or barrel, providing a stable rest for the rifle when it is not actually in use. If the rest is correctly positioned on the firing-point in front of the firer, the rifle can be lowered into it between shots. This is more convenient and safer than placing the rifle on the ground, especially in wet weather. The better type of rests have plastic covered forks and, for those who value a nicely polished rifle, this is the type to use. Plain, and cheaper, rests can be rendered less liable to damage the polish on a rifle by binding the fork with cellotape or covering it with rubber tubing.

SCREWDRIVERS. Screwdrivers are very useful to have in the shooting bag and the gunroom locker. At least two are recommended; one should be large enough to check the main trigger-guard screws, and one sufficiently small to adjust the screws that hold the sight scales in position.

EAR DEFENDERS. Last, but by no means least, are ear defenders. Deafness is an 'occupational disease' among shooters and many, though perhaps not seriously affected, lose the ability to hear clearly the higher tones. Some, however, are made quite seriously deaf. Quite a number of well known shots have felt it prudent to give up shooting, the adverse effect on their hearing proving detrimental to their business interests. Most modern ear defenders and ear muffs are scientifically made, and their regular use cannot be too strongly recommended. The beginner should acquire the habit of wearing them from the commencement of his shooting career. There are several sorts from which to choose, from simple rubber or plastic plugs to more elaborate head-phone type muffs. The latter are made in two styles, one having a band over the top of the head and the other with a neck band for use when wearing a normal shooting hat. The latter are strongly recommended.

Note: Extract from N.R.A. Regulations (New addition for 1971)
All persons who intend to shoot or who are likely to be in close proximity when shooting is taking place are warned of the danger of damage to their hearing if they fail to protect their ears. They are strongly advised to wear ear defenders.

12

CARE AND CLEANING OF

TARGET RIFLES

If a high standard of performance is to be maintained, it is absolutely essential that the equipment used must be kept in perfect conditon. This applies to all pursuits which entail the use of mechanical aids and equipment but is particularly applicable to target shooting, where results depend so much on rifle and cartridge being completely in first class order. The firer can do little about the cartridge beyond following the advice given in chapter 6, but he should give considerable attention to his rifle. If neglected, the rifle—especially the bore—will deteriorate, with a consequent falling-off in accuracy. And it is reasonable to assume that if elementary cleaning is not properly carried out, other equally important operations in careful maintenance will also be neglected.

FOULING AND BARREL WEAR. For many years British Service cartridges were loaded with a hot-burning and erosive propellant —cordite—and an extremely corrosive cap composition. In addition, the combination of cordite with a flat-based bullet and consequent 'set-up' (chapter 2) added to the damaging effects. If careful and effective cleaning was not carried out very soon after firing, corrosion would set in and the barrel would rapidly deteriorate. In any case, even with maximum care, the erosion and wear factors restricted the target accuracy life of a .303 in. rifle barrel to somewhere in the region of 2,000 rounds.

Modern Service, and commercially made cartridges are mostly loaded with nitro-cellulose propellants. Where double-based powders are used, they are designed for the coolest possible burning. Cap or primer compositions are non-corrosive and most bullets are streamlined or 'boat-tailed'. All these developments minimise the damaging effects on the bore and in consequence barrel accuracy life is considerably prolonged.

As both types of Military cartridge are in regular use, and likely to remain so for some time, the effect of fouling and methods of overcoming it will be described for both. Before doing so, however, some explanation of what actually happens is necessary.

CAP FOULING. Certain types of cap composition contain substances which, after firing, undergo various chemical changes. They become hygroscopic and absorb moisture from the air, and they have an extremely corrosive effect on steel. Cap composition of the type used for many years in British Military cartridges contains potassium chlorate which, after ignition leaves depostis of potassium chloride in the bore. This has a great affinity to water and, if not completely removed after firing, will soon cause rusting. Modern primers of a non-rusting nature are now in general use, and so this problem will gradually be eliminated.

EROSION. This is the washing away of the bore by the hot gases generated by the ignition of the propellant charge. The actual temperature at this time is estimated to be between 2,000 and 3,000 degrees centigrade, depending on the propellant used. This has considerable effect on the steel surface, especially on that part of the rifling which is nearest to the chamber and cartridge. While the surface of the bore is being subjected to this great heat, it is also under considerable pressure from the propellant gases—in the region of nineteen tons to the square inch. If, in addition, the cartridge has a flat-based bullet which is 'set-up' by the explosive charge, further compressing effect is exerted on the vitally important first few inches of the bore. The combined effect of heat and pressure causing crumbling and fissuring of the surface with subsequent enlargement of the breech end—very little wear occuring at the muzzle. Erosion is not a form of fouling and nothing can be done to reduce its effect.

Similarly, wear caused by the friction of the bullet against the bore surface cannot be prevented. By comparison with erosion, it is not regarded as having a major effect on barrel life but is a factor which must be taken into account.

POWDER AND METALLIC FOULING. In the days of cupro-nickel bullet envelopes, metallic fouling (measurable and often visible lumps of cupro-nickel deposited on the rifling lands) was a serious problem. A rough surfaced barrel was particularly vulnerable, and older marksmen will have vivid recollections of barrels 'nickelling' and the drastic measures taken to remove it. The introduction of the gilding metal bullet envelope during the second world war—and in use ever since—has almost completely eliminated this problem. The only metallic fouling now occuring consists of coppery streaks which are sometimes visible in the muzzle end of rifle barrels. This has little or no effect on accuracy and is not difficult to remove. The only recent exception to this was with certain batches of Canadian .303 in. Mark 7 ammunition which had very soft bullets and tended to leave measurable deposits of metallic fouling.

With the .303 in. cartridge, powder fouling is regarded as of little importance, emphasis being on the thorough removal of the corrosive cap residues and the normal routine procedure for polishing out any metallic deposits. Such powder fouling as there is, disappears in the process.

In contrast, with modern cartridges powder fouling presents a much greater menace to accuracy than anything else. Modern nitro-cellulose propellants contain up to 10% of non-combustible matter in the form of stabilisers, graphite coatings and other additional constituents designed to control rate of burning, heat generated etc. A considerable proportion of this residue is left in the bore in the form of finely atomised dust. Another feature of British Service cartridges is that the bullet is sealed into the case by means of internal neck varnish, a black, somewhat thick substance which in its turn is deposited in the bore. The relatively gentle action of the streamlined bullet, which takes the shape of the rifling as the result of an interference fit rather than being forced into it, as was the flat-based bullet, results in the powder residues and neck varnish being rolled into the rifling grooves. This eventually builds up into quite considerable accumulations of fouling. It is probable that the fiercer action of the cordite loaded cartridge with flat-based bullet blasts out such residue each time a shot is fired.

This is of course mostly conjecture as it is difficult to prove exactly what goes on inside a rifle barrel, but there is no doubt whatever that unless the accumulations of fouling are throughly and frequently removed the effect on accuracy will be very marked—due presumably to the fact that the bullet is not seating fully into the rifling and may not be receiving its full spinning effect. As the fouling builds up, the conditions inside the bore are varying from shot to shot.

FOULING AND ITS REMOVAL. Cleaning a rifle barrel can be considered in four stages. They are:

   1. The use of a suitable solvent to soften or break up the fouling.

2. Polishing or scouring with mild abrasives or stiff brushes.
3. Swabbing and wiping out the bore until clean and bright.
4. Protection against rust by the use of grease or oil.

In the case of cartridges fitted with corrosive caps, such as the .303 in. Service cartridge, the fouling is soluble in water and the normal procedure is to pour three or four pints of warm water through the barrel, using a specially made funnel for the purpose. Warm water dissolves the fouling quicker than cold and has the additional advantage of heating the barrel, thus easing the process of drying the bore afterwards. The water should not be too hot as this could cause warping and other damage to the woodwork. When this method is not practicable, aqueous solvent—obtainable commercially—is an effective substitute. This is a mixture comprising one part of soluble oil to three parts of water. It is milky in appearance and is applied with a brush or on well saturated flannelette patches.

The fouling having been softened or dissolved, the next operation is to polish the bore. This also ensures the complete removal of all fouling. A mild abrasive applied on a tight fitting patch and given twenty to thirty double strokes up and down the bore will achieve this. A wire brush can be used for this purpose, phosphor-bronze being the least likely to harm the bore. Although this effectively removes fouling, it does not have the beneficial polishing effect of the tight-fitting flannelette patch and mild polishing compound.

The bore should next be swabbed out with cleaning-oil on patches, followed by dry patches until they come out reasonably clean, when the bore may be considered free from fouling. If a barrel is not completely clean when the rifle is put away, in addition to the risk of corrosion the process of wiping out in preparation for the next shoot is made more difficult. When the shooter is in a hurry, this pre-shoot cleaning may be neglected. If the rifle is not to be used the following day, the bore should be protected with oil or grease depending on the length of time elapsing before the next shoot.

In the case of cartridges fitted with non-corrosive caps such as the modern 7.62 mm Nato round, the cleaning process is similar but less arduous. More use can be made of solvents and there is less need for manual polishing and scrubbing, though occasionally this is necessary.

If commercially manufactured cartridges are used, the only fouling will be the powder residue which, though probably firmly established in the rifling grooves, can be relatively easily removed with a nitro-solvent of the amyl-acetate variety. This is applied with a stiff nylon or phosphor-bronze brush, passed up and down the barrel about ten or twelve times. It is not a bad thing to leave the solvent in contact with the barrel for a short while to give it time for maximum effect.

When cleaning out after using Service cartridges, and there is a possibility of neck varnish deposits as well as powder fouling, more drastic action is needed and a solvent applied on a phosphor-bronze wire scourer is effective. An occasional polish with a mild abrasive on a tight patch is beneficial and should be carried out after about every fifty rounds.

Swabbing out, cleaning, drying and final greasing or oiling is as described for the .303 in. cartridge. A normal cleaning-oil will suffice if the storage period is short, but heavier greases are recommended if the rifle is being put away for several months. A wool mop should be kept exclusively for this task.

The face of the bolt can become damaged by escape of propellant gas and fouling from the cap. This takes the form of a ring encircling the striker hole. It can, in the main, be prevented if the bolt face is wiped clean and oiled after firing. Mauser and other front-locking rifles have recesses which are difficult of access at the forward end of the bolt-way. These should be regularly examined and kept clean by means of a patch on a screwdriver or something similar to ensure that they are free from oil before firing, and free from fouling and extraneous matter after firing.

The graduated scales of backsights and other external metal surfaces soon show signs of rust if not properly cleaned. A ¾-in. paint brush, dipped in one of the propietory cleaning oils—not solvents—can be used for these parts.

After cleaning and oiling it is beneficial to stand the rifle on its muzzle to allow any surplus oil to run out rather than soak into the woodwork around the action and, in time, probably causing it to soften and disintegrate.

SUGGESTED CLEANING SEQUENCE. Many different techniques can be employed, and probable changes in cartridge propellants, cap compositions etc., may affect present methods, but the following sequence applies to the majority of requirements:
1. Use of a solvent to dissolve fouling.
   (a) Water or aqueous solvent when using cartridges containing corrosive cap compositions and cordite propellant—such as the .303 in. round.
   (b) Nitro solvent when cartridges have nitro-cellulose propellant and non-rusting caps.

2. Polishing or scouring. Use of mild abrasive recommended in preference to metal brushes. Either will break up and remove hard fouling. The mild abrasive has a polishing or lapping action which the wire brush does not.
3. Removing of fouling and polishing compound with thin cleaning-oil on patch.
4. Thorough wiping out with flannelette patches.
5. Preservation of bore with oil or grease, depending on the time elapsing before the next shoot.
6. Attention to the bolt-face, sight scales, and other metal parts and woodwork.

GAUGES AND GAUGING. A barrel gauge is used to determine the bore diameter of a barrel, to ascertain whether it is reasonably parallel, and to detect fouling. The gauge is pushed through the bore from the breech end by means of a rod. When screwed on a rod, a gauge should only be held by one or two threads so that it is free to wobble as it moves along the bore. This ensures that it is not forced against the rifling at an angle, which might result in damage to the rifling. Barrel guages should always be used with extreme care for this reason.

Although barrel gauges are essential to a gunsmith or armourer, there are few occasions when a marksman has any real need to apply them. Should such an occasion arise, however, the following are the chief points to bear in mind:

1. A gauge of the same size as the diameter of the bore will detect the slightest variation in bore size.
2. When a gauge of the correct bore diameter seems to move in jerks down the length of the barrel, it may give the impression that the bore is uneven. In fact, the gauge is probably nearly an interference fit and is showing up microscopic unevenness which may be as little as .0001-in. and can have no effect on accuracy.
3. A gauge that passes smoothly down the barrel gives the impression that the bore is level. This may not be entirely true, for if the gauge is a fraction smaller than the bore in diameter it will not detect small variations.
4. A tight-fitting gauge can scratch and score the bore to such an extent as to render the barrel completely unserviceable, and can become stuck in the bore if forced against slight obstructions.
5. A gauge only indicates the diameter and regularity of the bore, i.e. across the lands. It gives no information regarding the grooves which in modern barrels comprise more

than half of the surface of the bore and are of equal, if not greater importance.

From the foregoing it will be appreciated that unless barrel gauges are correctly and intelligently applied they may only add worries and troubles to the user. Many barrels have been spoilt, sometimes at the muzzle end where sharply defined rifling is of extreme importance, through attempts to scour out imaginary fouling which was really only slight unevenness of the bore.

MEASUREMENT OF BARRELS. As already stated, a barrel gauge gives no information on the vitally important groove diameter. The method used by gunsmiths for checking this is by a cast lead bullet several thousandths of an inch larger than the bore diameter of the barrel to be gauged (a .32 in. bullet is suitable for a 7.62 mm barrel). By means of a rod, this is pushed through the barrel from breech to muzzle. As the lead slug passes through, tight and loose spots can be noted for subsequent action, such as lapping. The lead slug can then be carefully retrieved from the muzzle and measured by a micrometer. This will provide information as to the groove diameter at the smallest point and in consequence will be of limited use as a guide to wear at the breech end. It is wise to protect the bore with a film of fine lubricating oil before pushing through the lead slug.

LAPPING. 'Lapping' is the term applied to polishing the bore with a lead plug cast to fit the individual barrel. The initial gauging sometimes indicates a tight spot in a bore which is otherwise level; or there may be a rough patch in a barrel which in other respects is perfect. These can be corrected by lapping, and the method of making a lead lap is as follows:

1. Burn off the bristles from an otherwise useless bristle brush. Wrap a small twist of tow around the junction of the brass section of the brush and the wire.
2. Push a cleaning-rod, with modified brush assembled, into the barrel of the rifle from the breech end so that the tip of the wire is an inch or so inside the muzzle. Stand the rifle upright on its butt.
3. In a suitable ladle, melt sufficient lead and pour it steadily into the muzzle until that end of the barrel is completely filled. Leave it to cool.
4. When cool, push the rod forward, revealing the newly cast lead lap. Saw off the rough end with a hacksaw and the lap is then ready for use.

   Depending on the amount of polishing required, use a

suitable polishing compound or abrasive on the lap to achieve the desired result. The best to use is a proprietary brand of polishing paste containing diamantine. Very fine carborundum or old-fashioned knife powder is also suitable but a very strong abrasive should not be used.

THE STORAGE OF FIREARMS. Rifles should be stored in a dry place, preferably in some sort of gun cupboard with racks to take the rifles and shelves or drawers for cleaning equipment.

When a rifle is not going to be used for at least a few weeks, the bore should be protected with thin grease, which should also be lightly applied to the graduated sight scales and other metal parts. For shorter periods of time a normal cleaning-oil is adequate—but it should not be applied too liberally as it tends to soak into the woodwork. For this reason a thin grease is preferable to oil. As a further precaution the rifle can be stored muzzle downwards.

On no account should any cloth be in contact with the metal parts of stored firearms, and plugs of flannelette, or cotton wool etc., even if oiled, should not be inserted in the bore. They will eventually absorb moisture from the atmosphere and a surprising degree of corrosion can result from this practice.

When .303 in. No. 4 Rifles are to be stored for any length of time, it is beneficial to slacken the front trigger-guard screw one or two turns to reduce the tension on important bearing surfaces. A label tied to the swivel will act as a reminder to tighten it again before shooting.

CLEANING EQUIPMENT AND HOW TO USE IT. The normal cleaning requirements of a marksman have been described and the following hints on their use should be of assistance to the beginner:
1. It is an avantage to have two cleaning-rods, one of them with a jag permanently fixed in position so that it will not work loose and come off during cleaning operations. The other rod can be kept for the various other cleaning implements. A wooden rod-guide (figure 52, chapter 12) helps to prevent damage to the barrel lead when a steel rod is used.
2. The correct application of a 4 in. x 2 in. flannelette patch to the jag requires practice. The patch should be held diagonally in the left hand, the rod being held in the right (plate 58). The patch should then be firmly rolled on the jag, the end of the patch being turned over by the fore-

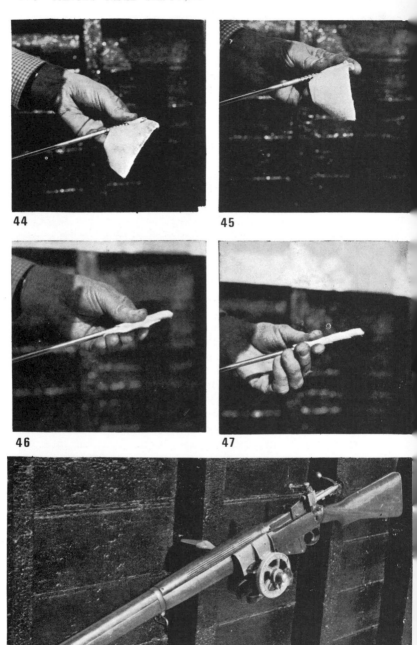

44

45

46

47

48

Plate 44. *Facing* Applying flannellette patch to cleaning-rod jag. Hold patch diagonally in the left hand rolling the corner tightly onto the jag. The rod is rotated with the right hand, and the patch rolled with the thumb and fore-finger of the left hand.

Plate 45. *Facing* Applying flannellette patch to cleaning-rod jag. With the patch still held firmly by the thumb and fingers of the left hand, turn the forward corner over the end of the jag with the fore-finger, still continuing the rotation of the rod with the right hand.

Plate 46. *Facing* Applying flannellette patch to cleaning-rod jag. Continue rolling the patch spirally and very tightly on the jag by turning the rod with the right hand.

Plate 47. *Facing* Applying flannellette patch to cleaning-rod jag. The patch correctly in position and ready for use. By repeating the process with each corner in turn, it is possible to use one patch two or three times.

Plate 48. *Facing* The 'Bisley' vice. A very useful item of cleaning equipment. Here, the vice, clamped to an upright pillar, holds a No. 4 rifle at an angle convenient for cleaning.

finger of the left hand (plates 59 to 61). By turning and reversing after it becomes dirty, a patch can be used two or three times. The patch should not be rolled on at right-angles to the jag or a jammed rod, with possible damage to the bore, will result.

Steel scourers are not recommended, but if they are used they should be inverted and fed into the bore from the muzzle end (figure 53). Wire brushes, if used, should be treated with care as they soon become damaged. Bristle and nylon brushes require little special attention. Wool mops should be kept exclusively for oiling or greasing barrels after the barrels have been cleaned; they should never be put into a dirty barrel.

3. When water is used as a fouling solvent, a funnel is the best means of getting it into the bore. Suitable funnels are available commercially and most club gunrooms are equipped with one or more. Those who wish to make their own can do so at modest cost, using an ordinary polythene domestic funnel, a short length of rubber tube and a cartridge case with the base sawn off. In an emergency, when no funnel nor aqueous solvent is available, the muzzle of the rifle can be placed in a container of water and, by using a cleaning rod and patch as a pump, water can be drawn up into the bore.

4. Any solidly constructed bench or table will serve for

cleaning rifles. If a vice can be permanently bolted to a bench it is a decided advantage. The jaws of a vice, which hold the rifle butt, should be protected with cork or felt clams so that the rifle is not damaged, and the fore-end

Fig. 53. Showing method of feeding wire scourer into muzzle of rifle. If it is accidentally withdrawn from the breech during use, it must be removed from the rod and screwed on again at the muzzle end, and drawn into the barrel in the manner shown.

of the rifle should be rested on an armourer's 'horse' which is also a permanent fitting to a cleaning bench.

For those whose cleaning arrangements are of necessity less permanent, the vice illustrated in plate 62 is strongly recommended. It can be clamped to a table, tent pole or bench, and quickly removed after use.

PREPARATION FOR SHOOTING. The main points which should be attended to in the gunroom in preparation for shooting are:
1. Clean the bore with two or three dry, clean 4 in. x 2 in. flannelette patches and ensure that no oil is left in the chamber. Wipe the bolt, bolt-face, bolt-way and locking-lug recesses to remove all surplus oil, thus ensuring that none gets on the cartridge case.

The first shots fired through a barrel after cleaning are usually sighters on which the elevation for subsequent shots is based. The importance of stringent preparatory cleaning is therefore apparent. Whatever else is left undone, the chamber must be thoroughly cleaned and at least one patch put through the barrel before firing, if only to make sure that there is nothing in the bore that can in any way obstruct a bullet. A blob of grease, an excess of oil, or part of a cleaning patch, can cause a barrel to be completely ruined. When a bullet meets an obstruction of this nature, the sudden check induces a build-up of pressure behind the bullet causing the barrel to stretch or bulge. In the case of a total obstruction the barrel would almost certainly fracture. Even a small partial obstruction could render a barrel unfit for accurate target shooting.

2. Clean out the locking-lug recesses before replacing the bolt. Make sure that the bolt is the correct one for the rifle and that the serial numbers on bolt-handle and rifle body agree.

   In a crowded gunroom it is easy to pick up a wrong bolt and, as previously mentioned, bolts are not interchangeable. The differences which exist between one bolt and another are often quite sufficient to cause misfires or weak striker blows due to excessive headspace; variations of the rifle's zero due to ill-fitting recoil lugs; and, most likely of all, serious trouble with the trigger pressure. As a wrong bolt may appear to fit perfectly, the necessity to check the serial numbers when other bolts are lying around is obvious.

3. Check the important screws for tightness.

4. Check the backsight, making sure that the eyepiece is screwed in firmly. If, during firing, the eyepiece is loosened by the shock of discharge, it will gradually unscrew and give a slightly different line of sight for each successive shot. A shoot may well be ruined before this defect is noticed. Make sure the aperture is clear and the lens or filter—if any—clean. A misty or dirty lens is difficult to clean whilst lying on the firing-point. Set the sight at the elevation usually required for the range at which the rifle will be used, and ensure that the wind-scale is at 'zero'. Forgetfulness or carelessness in sight setting will result in misleading or wasted sighters.

5. Check that the foresight element is firmly held in position and is the correct one for the range. Also ensure that the supply of spare elements is in the shooting-bag in case a last minute change is necessary. Blacking foresights is now an operation of the past, but for those participating in competitions necessitating Service pattern foresight we would recommend the use of an acetylene (Carbide) lamp, which produces a deep, lasting black. Alternatively, the smoke from a square of camphor—kept in an air-tight tin is very effective, and easy to use and carry around. A blackened foresight should be covered with a fore-

sight protector.

6. Make sure that the telescope lenses are clean. In wet weather, water often gets inside the casing, causing the lenses to steam up through condensation—and they are not easily cleaned on the firing-point.

7. Before leaving the gunroom, a last-minute check should be made to ensure that one has all the items of equipment necessary for the shoot. The basic essentials are:

(a) Rifle, with correct bolt and sight-arm.

(b) Sufficient ammunition.

(c) Telescope and stand.

(d) Shooting bag or case, containing scorebook and pencil, register cards, spare foresight elements, duster or washleather etc.

(e) Groundsheet or wet weather clothing.

Some of the advice in the foregoing may appear to be very elementary but even the most experienced marksmen sometimes make foolish errors and omissions. It is always better to be 'safe' than 'sorry'.

13

TEAM SHOOTING AND TIE
SHOOTING

There are occasions in the shooting careers of most marksmen who participate in competitive shooting that are long remembered as having special significance. To be selected as a member of an important team, particularly for the first time, is such an occasion. Similarly, to find that one has tied for a first prize or for a place in one of the stages of a major competition, with the prospect of a shoulder-to-shoulder shoot-off, is not quickly forgotten.

The normal individual squadded competition has little or no spectator value; but in an important team shoot keen interest is displayed in individual performance by members of a participant's club, members of opposing teams, and the spectators who generally assemble for the closing stages of such matches. The tensions imposed upon a first class team shot are therefore obvious, and to build up a reputation as one takes time, determination and cool confidence. First experience in this direction may be in a school or rifle club team. Later would come county, regimental, provincial or inter-State matches; finally, as the ultimate goal, selection to represent one's country in matches of international status.

TEAMS AND MATCHES. A rifle team generally consists of a captain, from six to twenty shooting members and some reserves. International teams usually have in addition a non-shooting adjutant, whose job it is to assist the captain with administrative matters. In matches of less importance, the captain may also be a shooting member of the team.

A typical international match team would consist of eight firers, plus captain, adjutant, coaches and reserves. This is the normal make-up of teams taking part in such events as the Kolapore Match, which is annually contested at the Bisley National Prize Meeting between teams from Great Britain—known as the 'Mother Country'—and any country which is, or has been, part of the British Commonwealth or Empire, or any group (sanctioned by the N.R.A.) of such countries. In this match, Bisley's premier team event, each man fires ten shots at each of the 300, 500 and 600 yards ranges. The Empire Match, in which each firer has ten shots at each of 300, 600, 900 and 1,000 yards, is Australia's main international event. It has been contested at Bisley, in Australia and in New Zealand. Though open to all British Commonwealth countries, it can only be held when an Australian team is present. Owing to the relative infrequency of this match, participation is regarded as a considerable honour. The Rhodes Centenary Match, held in Rhodesia or South Africa, and the Canada and Commonwealth Matches in Canada, are similar events in which teams of international status compete.

In recent years, the U.S.A. has revived the Palma Match which was contested sporadically until the 1920's. This match which is open to teams of twenty, consists of fifteen shots fired at 800, 900 and 1,000 yards. It is customary for the host country to provide sufficient rifles and ammunition for all teams and this, together with the considerable amount of range accommodation required, inevitably limits the number of teams that can participate. The fact that 7.62 mm NATO cartridge is common to so many countries has undoubtedly been instrumental in reviving this interesting contest.

TIE SHOOTS. Tie-shooting—particularly when deciding one of the major events, such as the Queen's Prize at Bisley and the Governor-General's Prize in Canada—creates considerable interest and has a good deal of spectator appeal. A closely contested tie-shoot between top-class shots is well worth watching and for those participating it is a great test of ability and temperament.

SHOOTING IN A TEAM. Whether or not an event is important, if a shooter wishes to establish himself as a good team man he must do his very best, regardless of the status of the match. He can be reasonably sure that his performance will not pass unnoticed by those responsible for the selection of major teams. Captains of international teams are always on the look out for promising material and it is not necessarily the brilliant shots who win matches. The steady performers who can usually be relied on to produce a better-than-average score whatever happens, invariably have the match temperament. The really reliable team shots are therefore not always those who win first prize at important

CANADA

CAPTAIN LT COL BRERETON		EMPIRE					ADJUTANT CAPT MORGAN

	SS	1234567890	300	600	900	1000	TOTAL
SUSICK	43	4355454455	46	47	43	44	180
RICHEY	45	5555554344	50	46	37	45	178
PITCAIRN	44	5535454545	48	45	47	45	185
OUELLETTE	55	3543554444	46	47	46	41	188
DAINES	34	5534555445	47	49	47	45	188
SORENSEN	34	5545555355	48	41	44	47	180
HENNOK	44	5445444435	47	47	47	42	183
BUTTERFIELD	03	5554443554	48	46	48	44	186
		CANADA	380	368	359	353	1460
		GT BRITAIN	376	367	358	3	1101
		AUSTRALIA	380	369	367	3	1116
SOUTH A 1115		N RHODESIA	382	362	362	3	1106

0 1 2 3 4 5 6 7 8 9 CANADA

49

AUSTRALIA — 1964

EMPIRE MATCH	CAPTAIN A.S. HAY.	COACH W. MELLOWS.	ADJ.		
LEONARDI S	5544555555	48 900 455455535 5	46	179
BRADSHAW F	5455445454	46 900 344453443 4	35	178
RUSH R	445 555545	47 900 355545454 5	41	181
GIBBS D	4545545445	46 900 554455443 5	43	176
WOHLERS J	5445454544	45 900 344554553 8	45	177
WASLEY R	5455455455	47 900 465455555	48	186
THOMPSON E	5555455555	49 900 465554545 5	44	193
PATTINSON O	5555545454	48 1000 555545544	46	183
	5545454554	47 1000 455554544 4	46	
	5545455555	48 1000 445344544 5	42	
RANGE TOTALS	300 380	600 369	900 367	1000 337	TOTAL 1453
SUB. COACH					

50

Plate 49. The type of score-board used at Bisley for important team shoots. This board shows the individual shot by shot scores at 1,000 yards, and the totals at the other ranges, of Canada's winning team in the Empire Trophy match at Bisley in 1964. The scores of the opposing teams are also shown but when this photograph was taken they had not completed their shoot at 1,000 yards.

Plate 50. In the 1964 Empire Trophy match Australia finished in second place. On this board every shot at all four ranges is recorded. The Empire match is of Australian origin and only takes place when an Australian team is present.

meetings—though they usually figure well up in all the prize lists.

In the major team events, such as international matches, a marksman may not know until the day of the match whether he is shooting or whether he is one of the reserves. The young marksman, on finding his name included as a shooting member, may well plunge from pleased excitement to gnawing anxiety lest he make a mess of things and fail to jusify his selection. But he must not let these emotions disturb him too much. They are perfectly natural reactions. When the teams assemble on the firing-point he will gain considerable comfort from his familiar and respected coaches, who will give valuable advice and whose presence should have a steadying influence on his shooting.

A team shot should not be over-competitive. While he should always endeavour to make the highest score of which he is capable, striving for every possible point, it is not his job to concentrate on trying to make top score. If by chance he does, so much the better—but it should not be his objective. Somebody has to be low man and this is no disgrace—provided, of course, it does not constitute a crashing departure from current form or involve such inexcusable disasters as firing on wrong targets or going to pieces in the face of difficulties. It is the ability to rise above such things that makes the real team shot.

THE TEAM CAPTAIN. Team captains are usually chosen from senior marksmen who have themselves taken part in many team shoots and whose experience and personality are held in high esteem in the world of rifle shooting. In minor matches, however, such as between schools, rifle clubs etc., the captain may lack experience, and his anxiety to do well and not let down his team will no doubt be just as great as that of the most inexperienced member of his team.

By his conduct during a match, a captain can exert considerable influence on his team's performance. If he is overconfident, his team may regard the opposition too lightly and find itself unexpectedly beaten. If he is too pessimistic, he will soon have a dispirited team—and even if it eventually does well, his reputation with the members will diminish.

A good captain must do his best to inspire confidence, particularly in those he knows need it most—the inexperienced and those who are struggling hard to make a satisfactory score. Many a match has been won largely by the efforts of the lowest scorers who, in their struggle against adversity, have been saved from complete disaster by words of encouragement from their captain. A wise captain will ensure that the low scorers feel that their efforts were appreciated no less than those of the more successful. The top scorer is deserving of praise, of course, but not at the expense of those who did not fare so well.

TEAM SELECTION. Most rifle teams are picked by the team captain. In selecting teams for major events, such as international matches, he is usually assisted by his adjutant, and he may seek advice from other sources as well as obtaining information from official records. Current form as well as past performance plays a decisive part in helping a captain to choose his team.

Some teams are selected by the process of shooting for places, but this method has one big disadvantage. It sometimes happens that good individual shots who do well in a shoot for places are not good team men. In other words, they are 'misfits'. However good they may be individually, they sometimes have a disturbing effect on a team. This is particularly important in the case of a team which is to tour other countries, possibly for periods of several weeks. For such teams it is essential to select men who will not only get on happily among themselves but who are good mixers and will not create misunderstandings or leave bad impressions on the people they meet on tour. These characteristics are almost as important as the ability to do well on the ranges; and it is generally found that, as the tour develops, young shots who have shown promise before they left home improve and shoot brilliantly, encouraged and inspired by their more experienced team mates and the high class opposition which invariably confronts them.

Anyone who has had the good fortune to be a member of a touring team, and who has enjoyed the good fellowship which invariably exists not only in the team itself but also with the shooting men of other countries, will appreciate the care that is needed in team selection. It is a source of considerable satisfaction to a captain to see his selection justified, and it is equally satisfactory to the team member to produce results justifying his selection.

Team selection is not always an easy job, especially when there are plenty available to choose from. Invariably there are some who, by virtue of proven ability as team shots are an automatic selection, but completing the team is often the real problem. As has already been stated, some shots who are consistently successful in individual competitions can never find their best form in a match no matter how often they are selected, and there are some who can always be relied on for a reasonably good score in a match but seldom shine in individual events. A very slow shot, however good he may be, can be a nuisance when the team is shooting to a time limit. Apart from the effect his dalliance may have on his coach or shooting partner, he may be the cause of the last firers having to hurry and 'shoot against the clock'—possibly losing valuable points in the process.

These are just a few of the many considerations which need to be taken into account when selecting a team. But in the final analysis, perhaps wholehearted team spirit is the most essential ingredient.

FIRING-POINT PROCEDURE. In a well organised team, adjutant, coaches, shooting members and reserves all have their tasks to perform, in which they should be well briefed before the match.

Having accomplished his main job of team selection, the captain can concentrate on leadership and encouragement to his team, leaving the administrative details to his adjutant.

The reserves are usually made responsible for issuing the ammunition to the firers on the firing-point and checking that sights have been set to the correct elevation. This check is of special significance since in most team matches only one sighting shot at each range is allowed. Tasks such as marking the score boards are also generally carried out by the reserves. Examples of team score boards are shown in plates 49 to 51. Comparatively small errors in sighting can result in missed targets when firing at long ranges so they are sometimes employed to keep careful watch for the strike of the first shots of each firer. If the target is missed, the strike of the shot on the stop-butt is located—and it can usually be seen through a telescope—the necessary sight correction can be made to bring the next shot on to the target.

The team captain will decide on the coaching procedure to be employed and make his dispositions accordingly. He will probably discuss the matter with his team members and find out if they have individual preferences for any particular method of coaching, guided by the knowledge that his team will better acquit itself if the members shoot under the conditions and circumstances which are to their liking.

The captain will also have to decide—and to some extent his decision will be influenced by the method of coaching he uses— whether or not his team will shoot singly or in pairs. Some firers like to shoot alone and some prefer a partner. With a very inexperienced team, it is better for the captain to make his own decision rather than consult the firers on the aspect of team procedure on which they probably know very little. When the team is composed of top-class experienced shots, however, he will be well advised to obtain their views.

When shooting singly, it saves time if each successive firer establishes himself on the firing-point quietly and efficiently before his predecessor has finished his shoot. He is then ready to commence without any delay, and his coach—if lying beside the firer—can quickly move over to his new position without losing touch with the wind. Time saving is an important factor in team matches when a strict time limit is imposed.

It is customary for a chart or diagram giving the names of the firers and coaches or sub-coaches on each target, the time of assembly and other important and necessary information, to be displayed on notice-boards—when available—well in advance of the commencement of the match. If this is done, all concerned will have no excuse for ignorance of any matter concerning the match. Some captains give each member of their team a card bearing all the relevant information. Detailed 'operation orders' are unnecessary, but some preliminary briefing and discussion is advisable.

COACHING. Under the rules governing team matches in the United Kingdom and in most Commonwealth countries, coaches to assess and call the wind allowance for their teams and generally advise the firers are permitted. In most minor matches, such as inter-club shoots, it is usually the captain and the experienced team members who carry out these duties. But in the more important events, particularly in international matches, each team usually has a main coach with a powerful telescope in a central position on the firing-point and sub-coaches sitting or lying close to the firers.

The function of the main coach is to watch the wind flags and/or mirage and assess the wind's strength and direction. This information is passed on to the firers as quietly as possible so as not to disturb them, by the sub-coaches. The sub-coaches operate in close liaison with the firers and, besides passing on the main coach's wind call, give advice on any sight adjustments considered necessary to centre the individual's group on the target. By keeping a careful diagram, a sub-coach should at all times have a clear picture of how his firer's group is forming— and this can only be achieved if the firer is frank with his coach and not afraid to admit when a shot is a bad one.

An alternative to the central coaching system is for the team members to fire singly, each having a target to himself and a coach at his side to concentrate solely on giving advice on wind, etc. Experience has shown this to be the most efficient method and is much favoured by the Australians and New Zealanders, who are among the most successful team shots in the Commonwealth. They even go to the length of allowing the coach to make sight adjustments on the firer's rifle to avoid the firer being disturbed by having to do it himself. In these circumstances, the sub-coaches become the wind coaches and the main coach has very little to do besides keeping an eye on the overall wind and weather conditions and being available for consultation in cases of uncertainty.

Opinions differ as to whether a coach should give orders or only advice. It should largely depend on the experience or otherwise of the firers. Successful coaching often comes from a combination of both.

A coach, though keeping careful watch on wind-flags and/or mirage, must also give some attention to the firer and his rifle and equipment. There are many things that can go wrong—such as eyepieces working loose or sight adjustments made in the wrong direction—for which a coach should be on the alert. Every possible encouragement should be given to the firer by his coach in a way that is compatible with the individual's temperament.

A good coach will not get rattled and will remain calm and imperturbable however badly a match seems to be going.

The question of whether the coach should keep the scorebook diagram of the firer and whether the latter should use his telescope to see the position of his shots on the target frequently crops up, and is subject to the whims and fancies of the team captain, coaches and firers. It is considered inadvisable to lay down a hard and fast rule on this matter. While some firers prefer to concentrate on holding, aiming and firing and leave everything else to their coach, others prefer to take a more active part in the proceedings, such as keeping their own diagrams and consulting with their coach on allowances for wind. Much depends on the experience of those concerned, and it is preferable to allow shooters and coaches to operate the system that they know will best suit their individual requirements. One thing is certain: a coach cannot keep his eye glued to the telescope in fast-changing wind and look after the firer's score book at the same time.

FIRER AND COACH. Whatever method of coaching is employed it is imperative that there is a real understanding between coach and firer and that the firer has every confidence in the man who is looking after his interests. In his early team shooting experiences, the young marksman should place himself unreservedly in the hands of his coach or sub-coach and do exactly as he is told. He can safely do this if he knows his rifle is correctly zeroed. If he has previously absorbed and acted on the principles of zeroing and grouping (chapter 7), when his coach tells him to put a certain wind allowance on his sight he can do so without a qualm. A young aspirant to team success will learn far more by doing as he is told and will usually make far better scores than if he tries to be groundlessly assertive and opinionated. In fact, he will quickly find himself omitted from teams—however good he may be—if he acquires a reputation for being unco-operative.

To the really experienced shooter, the coach becomes more of a companion on the firing-point; and, to the coach, appreciating that his firer's knowledge and experience is almost equal to his own, coaching becomes largely a form of consultation between experts.

A team shot should endeavour to shoot quickly. Nothing is so irksome as having to change the wind allowance several times in the process of firing a single shot. Not only is it likely to result in a bad shot being fired in sheer desperation, but firer and coach will eventually lose the mutual confidence which is so essential to success.

Wind should always be called in minutes of angle with direction given as 'right' or 'left'. Elevation readings should also always be referred to in minutes of angle. When sights are checked, as they invariably are before the beginning of an important match, the checker will expect the firer to refer to his elevation in 'minutes' and not in 'clicks'. This may seem relatively unimportant, but wrong calls can easily lead to confusion and lost points.

Really good coaching gives a team a great advantage, but it is imperative that the coaches are men of experience and that a feeling of mutual confidence prevails between firers and coaches.

TIE-SHOOTING. A tie-shoot for an important trophy is one of the most exciting aspects of competition shooting. Normally, it consists of one sighting shot and three or five to count for score —followed, if necessary, by further individual shots until all but one contestant have been eliminated. In ties in which there are only a few contestants, each has a target to himself. In large ties, two firers will probably share a target firing alternately in the usual manner. When all have fired their alloted number of shots, the score-cards are collected and checked and all but the top scorer or scorers are eliminated and retire from the firing-point. If two or more are still in the tie, further individual shots are fired until a decision is reached.

In a tie-shoot a marksman's ability is really tested. It is not uncommon for an otherwise fine shot to be completely de-moralised by the prospect of firing a tie, but ability in this connection, invariably develops with experience. It is doubtful if the most successful and renowned winner of ties approaches the occasion without a feeling of trepidation: he would hardly be human if he did. It is the power to control the inevitable excite-ment and make the maximum effort coolly and calmly that brings success.

In tie-shoots in which there are a small number of firers, there is a great temptation to see what the opposing marksmen are doing. It is possible to see several targets through the backsight aperture and it is often hard to resist having a quick peep at what is happening next door. It is, however, far better to concentrate on one's own shooting. The man who can ignore what is going on around him and can shoot quickly and calmly is the more likely winner.

The ability to shoot quickly is an asset at any time, but it is particularly advantageous in a tie-shoot and many have been won by quick shooting. The temptation to fire quickly just for the sake of doing so, and as the result of nervous tension, must be resisted at all times. Speed without accuracy is useless, and it is better to fire steadily and get bulls-eyes than try to demoralise the opposition by shooting fast and probably scoring inners or worse.

Whether a tie-shoot is won or lost, it should be conducted with the utmost sportmanship and consideration. No tie-shooter worthy of the name would, for instance, start shooting until he could see that his opponent or opponents were also ready to commence. Little satisfaction would be gained from winning a tie by taking any sort of advantage over the opposition.

14

MATCH RIFLE SHOOTING

Match Rifle shooting is a specialised form of target shooting practiced solely in the United Kingdom. It is not confined to any particular design of rifle—though the conditions laid down are of such a nature as to keep the match rifle within the sphere of military use. At the same time, certain refinements and special sights are permitted which, in the past, contributed to its usefulness in the hands of skilled marksmen in the field of weapon and cartridge research. Match rifle shooting is conducted entirely at long ranges, the minimum distance in current competitive shooting being 900 yards, and it therefore requires the highest standards of wind judgement.

Apart from its fascination as a skilled sporting pastime, match rifle shooting was originally regarded as a medium for experimental work in connection with the development of small arms and small arms ammunition. A fitting reference to this work was made by the President of the War Office Small Arms Committee in his report of the Bisley Imperial Meeting of 1921. He stated:

'The Match Riflemen competing at Bisley—about 60 in number—specially interested in accuracy at 900 to 1,200 yards, and having behind them some 60 years experience in this class of rifle competition carried on under the arrangement of the N.R.A., has had a definite bearing on the progress of the rifle and has afforded an unofficial and open field for trial of new methods and devices without expense to the Public'.

Over the past hundred years the records of the development of British military rifles and cartridges provide many instances of practical assistance from the trials and experiments of match rifle marksmen. Although the description 'match rifle' was not in general use in British competitive target shooting until the end of the nineteenth century, it is probably true to describe match rifle shooting as the earliest form of competitive rifle shooting. In the nineteenth century, match rifle shooting was also conducted on similar lines in the U.S.A.

By its very nature, match rifle shooting is restricted to a relatively small number of participants and the ranges on which it can be carried out are few. The supply of special sights is also somewhat limited as they are uneconomical to manufacture. The availability of ranges and sights, however, has been just about adequate to satisfy the demand.

HISTORICAL OUTLINE. At the early Imperial Prize Meetings at Wimbledon certain competitions, mostly long distance events, were open to what was known as the 'Any Rifle' class. This class provided for the private experimenter, usually gentlemen of wealth, and for the gunmaker to test his new designs. Rifles in this class were also referred to as 'small bores', their calibres, around .45 in., being considerably smaller than the .577 in. Service arm.

The 'Any Rifle' prize lists of the first few Wimbledon Meetings were largely dominated by the Whitworth rifle, which was much more accurate, especially at long range, than the British Service arm of the day, the Enfield muzzle-loader. The years immediately preceding the first Wimbledon Prize Meetings were marked by an important step in rifle development; the experiments of Sir Joseph Whitworth establishing the main principles on which the small-bore rifle was founded. In 1854 his aid was sought by the British government in investigating the mechanical principles involved in making the best possible rifle for military use. Briefly, the result of Whitworth's experiments was a muzzle-loading rifle of .45 in. calibre, embodying hexagonal rifling with a twist of one turn in twenty inches as opposed to the Service Enfield's rifling of one turn in seventy-eight inches. The Whitworth fired a lead bullet cast to the same cross-sectioned shape as the bore, and the 'Any Rifle' class at Wimbledon provided the means for critical accuracy assessment. There can be no doubt that British rifle manufacture greatly benefited from the processes and accurate tools introduced by Whitworth, and, as a result of his efforts, long distance target shooting became a practicable proposition several years earlier than it would otherwise have done.

Meanwhile, another great pioneer of British rifle development—a civil engineer named William Ellis Metford—was carrying out experiments which were to have far-reaching results and considerable influence on match rifle shooting. He made many important discoveries in connection with the movement of rifle barrels resulting from the shock of discharge, and designed a ballistic pendulum for ascertaining the velocities of

Plate 51. The type of board used in the National match. This was England's winning team in 1966. Seated immediately behind the centre of the famous National Challenge Trophy is the team captain, Lieut. A. G. Fulton M.B.E., D.C.M., the only man ever to win the King's Prize three times.

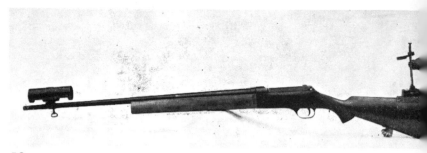

52

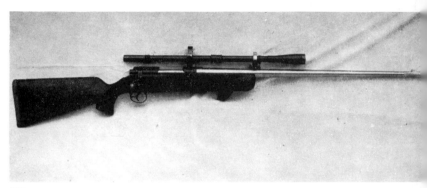

53

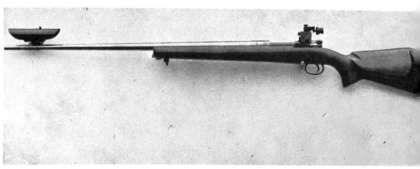

54

Plate 52. Conventional back position match rifle.

Plate 53. Match rifle for prone position shooting with telescopic sight.

Plate 54. Match rifle for prone position shooting with magnifying optical sights.

bullets. Among the many conclusions he arrived at regarding rifling and bullets was the fact that shallow grooving and hardened bullets gave by far the most satisfactory results. This disproved the long-held theory that deep grooving and soft lead bullets were necessary for accurate shooting. The principles of Metford became generally accepted and the Whitworth and similar rifles found themselves outclassed in the 'Any Rifle' events at Wimbledon.

In 1897, the term 'Match Rifle' superseded that of 'Any Rifle'. That year the Lee-Metford Rifle, adopted by the British Regular Army eight years earlier, was issued to the Volunteers and came into general use at the Imperial Prize Meeting, now held at Bisley. It was .303 in. calibre—much smaller than its predecessor—and in view of the virtual end of large bore rifles in the armed forces the Match Rifle class, hitherto with a maximum calibre of .450 in., now had to be brought into line with military requirements. What now became the match rifle was rather more military in character than its predecessors, and the maximum calibre was fixed at .305 in. This was later amended to a nominal calibre of .303 in.

It now became possible to fit suitable sights to the Service rifle and use it in match rifle competitions. Although this had the effect of bringing in a few more adherents to long range shooting, the match rifle had outstripped the Service arm in accuracy. Match rifle shooting, however, now became less a fashionable pastime for people of means and more a democratic one for a comparatively small body of real enthusiasts.

In 1901, the .256 in. Mannlicher rifle won nearly all the first prizes in the match rifle events at Bisley and was, for a few years, the favourite rifle. It was cheaper than most other match rifles and excellent ammunition was available for it. The light bullet, however, was easily deflected by wind and in rough weather the .303 in. more than held its own. Two years later, with new cartridges made by the Kings Norton Metal Co., the .303 in. rifle came well to the front again in the hands of the few who used it. For the next few years the provision of Kings Norton cartridges gave the .303 in. rifles a pre-eminence over the .256 in. Mannlicher.

In 1910, the pointed Mark 7 bullet was adopted for the British armed forces and about ten years later was in general use at Bisley. It had a higher velocity than its predecessor and needed less allowance for wind.

After the First World War an important change was made in the match rifle rules and only barrels of nominal .303 in. calibre were permitted. The next step forward in ammunition development was the streamlined bullet, and the important role played by match riflemen in this connection has already been mentioned. Serious thought was being directed to the possibility of a high velocity rifle for the British armed forces and, with this in mind, much experimental work was being carried out in the evolution of a suitable cartridge. Eventually, the .303 in. magnum cartridge, developed by the Imperial Chemical Industries at their Kynoch works at Birmingham, made its appearance. The development of this cartridge provided much evidence of the benefit accruing from the intensive annual tests at Bisley by the match riflemen. Up to and including 1925, this cartridge often gave extremely wild shooting; but the information gained in this period led to the introduction in 1926 of a streamlined bullet which solved many of the problems previously experienced.

When the interest in a high velocity rifle for the armed forces receded, it became unnecessary to pursue work with the magnum cartridge, and thoughts were directed towards a cartridge of the same dimensions as the Mark 7 but with a streamlined bullet. The outcome was the Mark 8Z cartridge with nitro-cellulose propellant, which was eventually adopted by the British armed forces principally for use in machine-guns.

From 1933 until the introduction of the 7.62 mm cartridge in 1964 the streamlined .303-in. bullet in a normal Service cartridge case has been used for match rifle shooting. Special cartridges, subsidised by the manufacturers, being made available each year by the Metals Division of Imperial Chemical Industries Ltd, who were unsparing in their effort to provide ammunition of the highest possible standard of accuracy.

In 1964, after an unsuccessful start using Service quality 7.62 mm NATO ammunition in the newly converted Match Rifles with disastrous results, specially made M.R. cartridges with 185-grain streamlined bullets were imported from the Raufoss factory in Norway and from F.N. in Belgium. The performance of this type of ammunition seems to be comparable with that of the best .303-in. streamline.

THE MATCH RIFLE. Under existing rules, any breech-loading rifle may be used provided it is sufficiently strong to support the relatively heavy barrel and withstand the pressure generated by the cartridge. Most conventional match rifles are built on the better types of Continental military actions, such as the Pattern 1896 Mannlicher and the 1896 and 1898 Mauser. A standard type of barrel must be fitted. The Pattern '14 Rifle, which is a modified Mauser of British design, is also fairly popular and, of recent years, a number of match rifles embodying B.S.A. sporting rifle actions of modified Mauser design have been in use. Some of the latter were made with a solid floor, i.e. without a magazine opening. For official definition see Appendix 1.

Up to and including 1963, the .303 in. match rifle barrel, which had a maximum weight of $3\frac{1}{4}$ lbs, was used. This had 4-grooved rifling, designed with a short bullet lead and appropriate groove diameter to suit the streamlined bullet. From the commencement of the 1964 season, the 7.62 mm cartridge took the place of the .303 in. round and a new barrel of greater weight was adopted. This also embodies 4-grooved rifling.

The majority of match rifles, being intended for shooting in the back position (fully described later in this chapter), are made with short fore-ends, the barrel being exposed and unsupported from the reinforce forward. The fore-end of the stock must be of sufficient length to rest on the firer's knee when he assumes the back position. Extensions, or 'knee-boards', can be fitted for this purpose.

Examples of match rifles are shown in plates 52 to 54.

SIGHTS, CONVENTIONAL. The backsight is of the tangent type, with vertical and lateral adjustment. Some backsights embody a clicking device giving definite half-minute movements, similar to those in use on Target Rifles, but a large proportion of the older ones lack this refinement and corrections have to be made by reading the graduated scales. To make adjustments more difficult there is no standardisation in sight movement, some sights embodying right-hand threads and some left-hand. Thus, in order to apply lateral deflection, it is necessary to turn the adjusting knobs clockwise on some sights and anti-clockwise on others. This can be confusing to the owner of two or more rifles whose sights are not identical in this respect. In order that the eyepiece may be as near as possible to the firer's eye when he is in the back position, the backsight is mounted on the heel of the butt. This gives a considerably increased sight radius with a consequent reduction of aiming errors.

The foresight is invariably of an optical type of low magnification which, when used in conjunction with a minus clearing lens in the backsight aperture, produces a simple Galilean teleseope of approximately two to three magnifications. The foresight itself is usually a ring painted on the front lens (plate 69), the inside diameter of which must be sufficient to allow a clear view of the aiming-mark at all normal match rifle distances. Some marksmen prefer a cross reticle (plate 70) and in aiming with this type of foresight the target is quartered.

As will be seen from the various illustrations, the foresight is a somewhat cumbersome element fitted with a shade to keep rain from the lens. In addition, it has a spirit-level incorporated to assist in keeping the rifle upright. The foresight is normally located on a lug or projection on the barrel which fits into a recess in the underside of the sight. The complete assembly is clamped in position by a hand-operated screw.

It can be logically argued that to attach one sight to the barrel of a rifle and the other to the woodwork is not a sound mechanical practice, and the somewhat tenuous manner in which barrel and woodwork are sometimes held together provides considerable substance for this supposition. However, in spite of this—and the fact that many match rifle sights in use are extremely antiquated and have quite alarming amounts of looseness and backlash in the threaded portions—the scores made with them are remarkably good and perhaps indicate that undue fussiness in these matters is sometimes unnecessary.

SIGHTS, TELESCOPIC. Any type of telescopic sight is allowed in match rifle shooting, the majority of users firing from the prone position. Most of the telescopic sights used for this purpose are of the simple tubular type, containing adjustment for focus and for the elimination of parallax. They generally embody cross-wire graticules, which are popular for most forms of target shooting. The actual adjustment for sighting is invariably external and incorporated in micrometer adjusting heads in the rear mounting, the front mounting being flexible to allow the tube to move (plate 57).

Opionions differ as to the amount of magnification desirable in a telescopic sight to give the best results for target shooting. There is, however, no doubt that the more powerful the tele-scope the more it magnifies the firer's holding errors, in addition to reducing the field of view. A reasonable magnification for match rifle shooting is 12X, but it is really much a matter of personal taste. A factor of vital importance is that the telescope sight should be capable of removal and replacement without any alteration to the zero position.

Though not a simple matter, it is possible to fit a telescopic sight to a match rifle for use in the back position. There is, however, a definite risk that the firer may damage his eye as the rifle is not held as firmly as in the prone position.

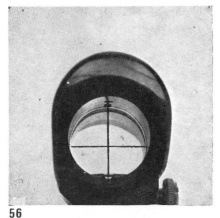

5

56

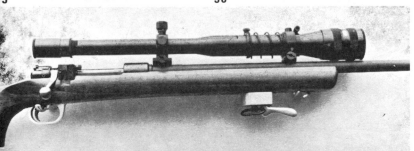

57

58

Plate 55. Match rifle optical foresight. A typical match rifle optical foresight, showing the ring reticule and spirit-level bubble.

Plate 56. Match rifle optical foresight with cross reticule, and spirit-level.

Plate 57. A popular type of telescope sight, positioned on a target rifle.

Plate 58. High telescope tripod. Long telescope tripod in position for spotting shots when the firer sits up. This also illustrates the head sling in use.

59

60

61

Plate 59. Firer sitting with feet towards the target.

Plate 60. Left foot under right knee. Weight taken on right hip. Note trousers tucked into sock, on left leg.

Plate 61. Rifle supported on bony part of right knee, which is firmly down on left foot. Butt pulled into right armpit. Weight taken on right hip, shoulder and elbow.

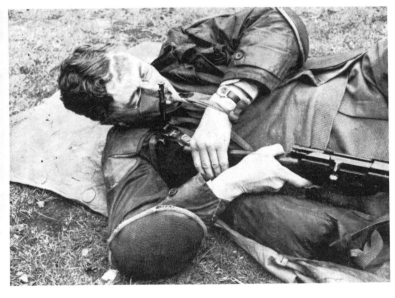

Plate 62. Supporting the head by means of a head sling which passes around the left leg. Length adjustment is rather critical.

Plate 63. Supporting the head with the 'teething ring' which is attached to the left wrist and held between the firer's teeth.

64

65

Plate 64. The head held up by muscular effort. No outside aids.

Plate 65. Supporting the head with the left arm. Fingers in contact with the ground. In this case the rifle is controlled solely with the right hand.

Although the telescopic sight is the most popular type for match rifle shooting in the prone position, it can be a source of trouble. Instances have occured when, due to the repetitive shock of discharge of the rifle, telescopic sights have gone completely out of adjustment. When this happens, the unfortunate firer will most probably miss the target, and go on missing it—for emergency repairs are seldom possible.

SIGHTS FOR THE PRONE POSITION. An alternative to the telescope sight for the prone position is a variant of the conventional sight used in the back position. The foresight is similar, except that the ring is slightly smaller in diameter due to the shorter sight radius. In addition, it is desirable to have the centre of the ring so positioned above the bore as to keep the line of sight as low as possible.

The backsight generally used is of the standard Target Rifle pattern with half-minute clicks for elevation and lateral adjustment. The No. 4 or P.'14 rifle and Target Rifle sight is a very suitable combination for conversion to a prone position match rifle (plates 53 and 54). A normal negative (minus) clearing lens is fitted in the aperture, and the simple Galilean telescopic sight is thereby reproduced.

One small but very important modification sometimes introduced is that of an angled front lens which has the effect of 'bending' the line of sight by anything up to fifteen minutes of angle, thus reducing the backsight elevation by a comparable amount. In any case, a cheek rest on the rifle is generally required to support the face and keep the eye in the correct relative position to the backsight aperture when it is elevated for the long ranges used in match rifle shooting.

THE BACK POSITION. The back position has always been in general use in match rifle shooting. From a purely target shooting viewpoint, this position has much to commend it, particularly as the objective is a sustained high standard of accuracy at extreme ranges. Its main advantages are:

1. The long sight radius, which is an important factor towards eliminating errors in aiming. The overall length of the average match rifle is about 54 inches and it is possible to utilise most of this to give a maximum sight radius. This is generally in the region of 48 inches—which is much longer than if the rifle was used in the prone position, the sight radius of, for instance, the P. '14 Rifle as used for target rifle shooting being about 32 inches.

2. Being in close contact with the armpit and resting on the knee at the fore-end, the rifle is supported for the greater part of its length by the firer's body.

3. Most match rifle competitions consist of long series of shots, fifteen or twenty being fired at each range, and this can become a wearisome business. The back position allows a firer to sit up and relax between shots, which he cannot so easily do in the prone position. With a spotting telescope mounted directly over the firer on a high (3 ft.) tripod (plate 58) he can spot his shots on the target from the more comfortable sitting position and, at the same time, ease his back.

Preliminary considerations. For comfort, all keys, pocket knives, loose change, etc., should be removed from the right-hand trousers-pocket (for right-hand firer) before assuming the position. If left in the pocket, they may finish up beneath the hip bone, causing pain and consequent loss of concentration, which will have a bad effect on accuracy.

No special padding is required on the shooting coat, though a leather patch on the right elbow may be helpful. It is certainly desirable to tuck the end of the left trousers-leg into the top of the sock, otherwise it gets in the way when aiming. Alternatively, some form of knickerbockers, plus-fours, or loose fitting breeches can be worn to advantage.

The firing position should be arranged so that the muzzle of the rifle is forward of the line of number-pegs on the firing-point. It should always be remembered that it is inconsiderate to lie so far back that one's muzzle-blast can cause discomfort to one's neighbours on the firing-point, especially those firing in the prone position. For the same reason, one should not take up more than a fair share of the firing-point.

ADOPTING THE BACK POSITION. Adopting the back position may at first seem a somewhat formidable process, but if taken step by step it soon becomes simple and habitual. For a right-handed firer the procedure is as follows:

1. With the rifle in the left hand, adopt a sitting position with the feet pointing towards the target, the weight being temporarily taken on the right hand (plate 59).

2. Raise the left knee so that the left foot is alongside the right knee and, at the same time, bend the right knee (plate 60).

6

67

Plate 66. A wrist rest in use with a telescope sighted Schultz & Larsen rifle.

Plate 67. Another form of wrist rest in use. The rifle is a modified P. 14.

3. Lie back until the right shoulder-blade is in contact with the ground, rolling over on to the right hip.
4. Place the butt of the rifle firmly in the right armpit and the fore-end on the bony portion inside the right knee. Place the right elbow firmly on the ground. Grasp the top of the butt with the left hand. The toe of the butt must *not* be in contact with the ground (plate 61).
5. Now take a general look along the line of sight to ascertain where the rifle is pointing. Errors in alignment must be corrected by pivoting the whole body and not by just moving the rifle. Adjustment in the vertical plane can be made by raising or lowering the butt in the shoulder and raising or lowering the right knee by turning the left foot under it. The foot, being conveniently wedge-shaped, can be arranged to give considerable variations in the elevation of the rifle. On no account should the knee be raised from its firm contact with the left foot to achieve this.
6. The head may be supported by the use of a head-sling (plate 62) or a 'teething ring' (plate 63). These two methods are recommended as being the most practical and least complicated for the beginner. Marksmen with strong neck muscles can hold up their heads without support and discomfort (plate 64). A few prefer to hold the rifle with the right hand only, placing the left hand around the back of the head (plate 65).

If the drill outlined above is followed, it will be relatively easy to adopt a position in which the eye will automatically align itself with the backsight aperture.

THE PRONE POSITION. The prone position varies little from that normally adopted for Target Rifle shooting. The main difference in match rifle shooting is that the firer is allowed the use of some form of wrist rest (plates 66 and 67). This is to offset the advantages of the back position, which is considered to give greater steadiness and less fatigue.

It is advisable to use a rigid rest that is either adjustable or has been specially constructed to give individual maximum comfort at the correct height. A rest made of wood, with felt or rubber padding on top, is the best type for the average person. Some firers use their shooting-bags, and a few have imported the expensive and relatively complicated machines used by the bench-rest shooters in the United States. It matters little which kind of rest is used—provided it serves its purpose. But a rolled-up coat, or something equally unstable, is definitely not recommended. When using a rest, remember that it is for the wrist or back of the hand holding the rifle. No part of the rifle may be in contact with the rest (plates 66 and 67).

The majority of prone-position match riflemen use a sling as well as a rest as an aid to holding. The combination is of doubtful value, and equally good results will be obtained with the rest alone. If a sling is regarded as essential, however, one of the single-point type—preferably the cuff pattern as extensively used by small-bore marksmen—will be found most convenient (chapter 9).

15

SHOOTING UNDER U.I.T. RULES

The Union Internationale de Tir or U.I.T. (often translated as International Shooting Union or I.S.U.) was formed July 17th, 1907, in Zurich, and is the controlling body for International and Olympic shooting.

SHOOTING AT STATIONARY TARGETS WITH THE FULL-BORE RIFLE. All the 'big' bore shooting is conducted at 300 metres with either the 'Free Rifle' or 'Big Bore Standard Rifle', the latter rifle having taken the place of the old 'Army Rifle'.

The Free Rifle is in traditional style with a thumb-hole stock and adjustable butt hook, a palm rest is permitted in the standing position only, if desired. Weight limit is 8 kg (17.6 lb) but trigger weight is not restricted. The Standard Rifle has a weight limit of 5 kg (11 lb) and a minimum trigger weight of 1.5 kg (3.3 lb). No butt hook or palm rest is permitted. Other maximum dimensions particularly those of the stock are controlled. The Standard Rifle may be shot in the Free Rifle competitions but not vice-versa. This rifle is very similar in many ways to the N.R.A. Target Rifle.

Both rifles have a maximum calibre of 8 mm, the most popular being either one of the 7.62 mm cartridges or the Swiss 7.5 mm. Of the 7.62 mm cartridges, the 7.62 mm x 51 and 7.62 x 53R have about equal following, the majority of shooters using whatever is or was their national military calibre. Other calibres are used in the hope of obtaining better accuracy or wind-resisting qualities. The usual 7.62 mm bullet weight is 185-200 grains though a lighter 168 gr bullet is used by some marksmen. These tend to suffer in a difficult wind.

RANGES AND TARGETS. All firing is done at 300 metres and ranges are so constructed that the shooter is protected to a fair degree from the wind. Some are of fine construction on multiple floors with superb facilities, others are of simple wood construction but provide the necessary protection and are adequate for the purpose. The target has a 10 ring of 10 cms diameter and each lower scoring ring is an additional 10 cms larger, out to the 1 ring which is 100 cms diameter. The 'black' or aiming mark is 60 cms and the minimum permitted size of the target is 1.60 metres high by 1.30 metres wide. An inner ten (X-ring) is 5 cms in diameter.

The course of fire is in three positions, Prone, Standing and Kneeling. 40 shots with 10 optional sighters are fired in each position with the Free Rifle and 20 shots with 6 optional sighters in each position with the Standard Rifle. Sighters may be taken between ten-shot strings. In the case of the Free Rifle a time limit is stipulated for each position with 15 minutes between, whereas with the Standard Rifle a $2\frac{1}{2}$ hour time limit for the whole shoot is imposed. The shooter may take what time he or she likes for each position within the overall time limit, but the positions must be shot in the correct order. The value of each shot is signalled as fired and patched with a transparent sticker. The complete target is changed after 10 shots and checked by 'Control'. The sighters are fired on a separate target which is indicated by a broad dark stripe printed diagonally across the upper right corner.

A register keeper sits behind the shooter to record indicated scores for spectator appeal and indicates to the butt personnel when the target should be changed.

SHOOTING POSITIONS. The three shooting positions have had considerable research devoted to them to ensure that they are technically correct. The bones, ligaments and muscles are used to their best advantage to produce for the individual shooter the most stable position coupled with one that is least affected by the pressure of competition, which in International events is considerable.

Those who participate successfully in these competitions are dedicated shooters devoting much time and effort to achieve perfection. Most practice is applied to the standing position, approximately 60—70% of training time being so utilised. Kneeling is next in importance whilst only 5—10% of time is spent in the prone position. Heavy expenditure on ammunition is not necessary as much beneficial training can be carried out by dry firing or the use of air weapons and smallbore rifles. A reasonable standard of physical fitness is essential not only for good shooting performance but also to help reduce nervous tension.

Some marksmen deliberately cant the rifle in order to obtain a more comfortable position and hold. While this is contrary to normally accepted practice, there can be no objection to it provided that the degree of cant is consistently maintained. As all firing is carried out at 300 metres the effect of canting is small in any case. (See The Effect of Canting on pages 99–104.)

THE PRONE POSITION. (Plates 68–69). In the prone position the shooter must strive for a perfect score. The World Record, set at Suhl in 1971, is 400. The full score of 200 has been achieved with the Standard Rifle although in this course of fire separate records are not recognised for each position.

The quality of rifles and ammunition has reached an extremely high level so most of the recent improvement in scores has come about by perfection of technique and mental attitude.

In adopting the prone position the angle of the spine to the line of fire should be between 5 and 20 degrees, the spine should be straight and the left leg approximately in line with the spine, with the foot being either vertical or turned inwards. The right leg is placed at approximately 45 degrees to the spine and moderately bent at the knee, with the right foot flat on the ground. This locates the right shoulder closer to the centre of the position, makes breathing easier, takes the pressure off the aorta, reduces pulsebeat and enables recoil to be absorbed more consistently.

The left arm is placed slightly to the left of the rifle. It is not desirable to place the elbow underneath the rifle nor too far out to the left. The left hand and wrist should be straight with the rifle rested on the heel of the hand and the fingers relaxed. The left forearm according to U.I.T. rules may not form an angle of less than 30 degrees from the ground. The sling which must be of the single point type with a maximum width of 40 mm, should be placed either high or low on the arm to avoid the pulsebeat from the brachial artery. The right elbow should be placed naturally with the right hand gripping the stock consistently, the only portion of the hand that moves for trigger operation being the first finger. The trigger finger should be clear of the stock and the first joint or pad should rest on the trigger. The butt plate should be close in to the neck and if an adjustable butt plate is used it should be raised to give maximum contact on the shoulder. Nearly all shooters with the free rifle use the butt hook prone.

The head should be held upright so that the organs of balance function efficiently and the eyes look straight ahead. If neces-

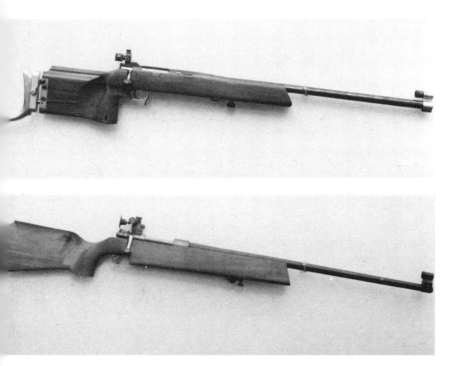

Plate 68.
Top U.I.T. 7.62 mm 'Free' Rifle with butt hook, thumbhole stock and set trigger mechanism.
Centre U.I.T. 7.62 mm 'Standard' Rifle built on Mauser '98 action.
Bottom Modern prone position. Note position of left elbow and left leg. Single-point sling used.

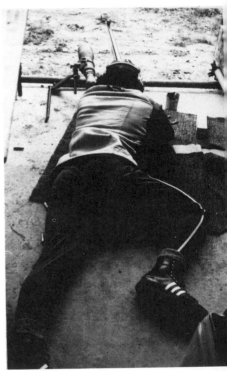

Plate 69.
Upper Modern prone position
showing position of right leg,
left arm and single point sling.
Lower Modern prone position
showing alignment of firer's
body and rifle. The right knee is
drawn up rather higher than is
normally considered to be
desirable though this is a
matter largely dictated by
individual conformation.

sary the rifle may be canted enabling the butt to be brought to the head, not vice versa. The eye relief must be maintained between 5 and 15 cms.

THE STANDING POSITION. (Plate 70). The shooter should stand approximately at right angles to the target with the feet about shoulders width apart, and the weight equally distributed thereon. The legs should be straight but the knees although having moderate tension should not be locked. The spine is bent back and twisted to the left. This back bend and twist begins above the hips which should remain level and in line with the feet. The left arm is rested against the rib cage and if the elbow reaches the hip bone it may be thus supported, however if it does not the rib cage will provide the support required and no attempt should be made to reach down to the hip bone. The left forearm should be relaxed and acts as a prop for the rifle. The left wrist should be in a natural position whether using the palm rest or resting the rifle directly on the hand. A variety of hand positions are suitable in the latter case but the rifle should not be rested on the finger tips as too many joints are involved.

The head should be held upright as in the prone position and the rifle should be so positioned that the head is bent slightly forward and downwards in order to see through the sights. The rifle is held considerably lower than was customary in the past when a very high position was favoured. This lowering of the rifle enables a lowering of the overall centre of gravity and gives a more 'solid' position.

The right arm is only used to get the right hand to the trigger and should be so positioned that only the trigger finger moves; the exact angle of the arm is not important but must be consistent.

The body-rifle combination is supported mainly by bones, and the centre of gravity of this combination should fall between the support area formed by the feet.

The World Record with the Free Rifle is 379 set at Munich 1972 whilst the highest score standing with the Standard Rifle at the most recent World Championships at Thun 1974 was 188 despite the much heavier trigger pressure required by the rules.

THE KNEELING POSITION. (Plate 71). According to U.I.T. rules the shooter may touch the ground only with the toe of his right foot, right knee and left foot. The use of a single point sling is permitted.

Plate 70.
Upper Rear view of standing position with U.I.T. rifle.
Lower Front view of standing position with U.I.T. rifle.

At the beginning kneeling can be extremely uncomfortable and unsteady but once a correct position has been developed it can be almost as steady as prone. Considerable effort and application is necessary to achieve this state of affairs.

To adopt the position the shooter should face approximately 75 degrees to the line of fire and kneel with his right knee on the ground and fairly well out to the right, sitting on his right heel. The right foot is perpendicular when viewed from the rear and the heel is placed at the base of the spine. A kneeling roll, which can be in a variety of sizes to suit individual requirements is placed beneath the right instep. For comfort the laces of the right boot should be loosened. The spine is vertical when viewed from the rear.

The left shin is placed vertically, with the left foot in line with the thigh or turned slightly inwards. The left elbow is placed on the knee, the forearm being in line with the left thigh. The point of the elbow should not be more than 10 cm forward of the bony surface of the knee and is slightly further to the left of the rifle than in the prone position. The left wrist is straight, the rifle being placed on the heel of the hand with the fingers holding the fore-end in a relaxed manner. The butt should be close to the neck and raised somewhat so the head can be held erect or slightly forward allowing the eyes and organs of balance to work efficiently. The butt length should be shorter than in the prone position and it should be remembered that it is not permissible to alter the length of the butt of the Standard Rifle after it has been passed by 'Control'. The left hand is closer to the trigger-guard than in the prone position and the sling shortened appropriately. The right arm has the same functions to perform as in standing and should be positioned accordingly.

The body conformation will dictate a variety of minor variations to suit individual requirements. In some cases it will be found more comfortable for the trunk to be erect, in others leaning forward. Similarly, some shooters prefer to adopt a low position dispensing with the kneeling roll altogether.

The World Record (kneeling) with the Free Rifle is 392, set at Pilsen in 1969, whilst the highest score with the Standard Rifle set at Thun in 1974 was 198.

Three-positional shooting under U.I.T. rules has not aroused a great deal of enthusiasm among British full-bore shooters at the present time. However, a new type of International competition to be fired in the prone position, probably at distances of 300 and 600 metres is currently under consideration, and this may well prove to have more appeal.

SHOOTING AT MOVING TARGETS WITH THE SPORTING RIFLE. This branch of target shooting is followed by a relatively small but increasing number of enthusiasts. It takes the form of shooting at a running deer target with full-bore sporting weapons, or at a running boar target using rifles firing .22 in. long rifle cartridges. The use of this particular cartridge is on the grounds of economy and also because the safety factors applicable to small-bore ranges are less complex than those of full-bore ranges. However, it is felt that mention of this aspect of target shooting is within the scope of this book.

THE RIFLE. As already mentioned .22 in. rifles are used. They may be single loading or be fitted with a magazine. The maximum total weight must not exceed 5 kilogrammes (approximately 11 lb). Telescopic sights are permitted and the majority of shooters use them, a magnification of 4X or 6X being most popular, though there is no definite ruling on this point.

Slings are not permitted, but adjustable butt plates are allowed within certain specifications.

From the foregoing remarks, it will be realised that the rifles used for shooting the running boar target are not sporting rifles in the strict sense. There is however nothing to prevent the use of weapons of more conventional pattern being used. Telescopes are however essential in order to aim off with the necessary degree of accuracy.

RANGES AND TARGETS. Running boar shooting is conducted on 50 metre ranges generally with a covered firing point. The target consists of a picture of a life-sized wild boar with scoring rings value 10-1 over the 'heart/lung' area, the 10 ring being 5 cms (2 in.) diam. Runs are made alternatively from left and right, a double target being used so that the one fired at is facing in the correct direction. The target is hidden from view except when crossing the 10 metres opening. It is operated electrically by remote control and 'fast runs' take $2\frac{1}{2}$ seconds to cross the opening, 'slow runs' taking 5 seconds.

Competitive shooting generally consists of 20 or 30 shot series fired at both slow and fast targets. Each series is divided into groups of 10 with 2 sighters. The value of each shot is marked as it is fired, and the target patched for each run.

SHOOTING PROCEDURE. Running boar shooting is conducted in the standing position, feet fairly close together and in the case of a right-handed shooter, the left side turned towards the

Plate 71.
Upper Kneeling position. Note left elbow forward of knee.
Lower Kneeling position. U.I.T. rifle. Note right foot directly beneath spine and supported by kneeling pad.

target. The butt is held close to the right hip to allow a smooth movement to the shoulder when the target appears (See Plate 72). As a result of experience and application, the firer will learn how much to aim off for fast and slow runs and also for different types of ammunition with differing velocities. It is essential that a smooth swing be maintained as the aim is perfected and the shot fired.

Much practice and attention to detail is required before any degree of expertise is achieved. Some running boar shooters make themselves scaled down ranges for use with air rifles at home in order to obtain the necessary practice. 'Dry' firing is always helpful and a reasonably high degree of physical fitness desirable as the long series of shots fired becomes very tiring.

GENERAL. This form of competitive target shooting has considerable spectator appeal as the scores and the progress of individual shooters can be recorded so that those behind the firing point can readily see how the contest is progressing.

Plate 72.
Top Anschutz .22 in. Running Boar rifle with telescopic sight.
Centre Running Boar target. Designed to be used from either direction.
Bottom The original Running Deer target, designed by Sir Edwin Landseer R.A., and first used at Wimbledon in 1863. Made of iron.

73

74

Plate 73. The Canadians' home at Bisley. Built in 1897 'Canada Hut' has since been the Bisley home of visiting Canadian marksmen. It stands at the end of an avenue of Canadian maples and over the main entrance is the head of a moose and the arms of the Dominion in colour.

Plate 74. An Empire match in progress on the Stickledown range. In the foreground is the Australian team, waiting their turn to shoot at 1,000 yards.

16

COACHING AND COACHING COURSES

No sport can continue to flourish and prosper without a steady influx of new blood. Target shooting is no exception to this generalisation, and schools, universities and cadet organizations are the most productive recruiting grounds. As in many other sports, a sound initiation into target shooting will have far reaching effects on any individual who has a desire to proficiency in marksmanship. To encourage potential marksmen and provide them with the opportunity to embrace the sport on correct orthodox lines, Rifle Clubs should be prepared with suitable coaching systems to give this service.

The National Small-bore Rifle Association gave the lead in this important matter some years ago by establishing a National Coach scheme for small-bore shooters, with very encouraging results, and the National Rifle Association is pursuing a similar course at Bisley for coaches and instructors in Target Rifle shooting. This lead could be followed with advantage by County Rifle Association throughout the United Kingdom. The result of sound initial training is often exemplified in junior competitive shooting such as in the Ashburton Shield contest, in which the school cadet teams with experienced instructors invariably fill the leading places.

COACHING COURSES. The object of this chapter is to outline the framework for elementary and more advanced coaching courses, applicable to beginners in target rifle shooting and providing some enlightenment on the subject to the coaches themselves.

It is obviously desirable for courses of this nature to be held on a rifle range, preferably equipped with a club-house or similar building that can be used as a lecture room. If sleeping accommodation is available, so much the better. The number of ranges so equipped is limited and consequently such courses could best be held at centres such as Bisley, Kingsbury (for the Midlands), Altcar (for the North), Dechmont (for Scotland),

and on a week-end basis. Smaller courses run by clubs or associations would probably be on a daily basis on a local rifle range. These could only be on the more elementary aspects of target shooting, with instructors from the more experienced members of the clubs concerned. Although necessarily limited in nature, they could prove most helpful to beginners.

While it is not possible to condense everything a beginner needs to know in a course lasting for only one week-end, it should not be overlooked that those under instruction are almost certainly keenly interested in shooting and therefore very receptive to learning as much as possible.

School Cadet Forces usually have a master with some target shooting experience in charge of shooting activities as well as a retired member of the Regular Armed Forces as permament staff. They can also call on the services of old boys of the school, many of whom would undoubtedly be willing to devote a little time to the assistance of the rising generation.

INSTRUCTORS. In theory, those best able to impart knowledge are those who possess it. In practice, however, those with the most knowledge are not always good at passing it on to others. It is therefore essential, if instruction on the somewhat technical subject of target shooting does not become dull and boring, for lecturers to be selected with considerable care both for their knowledge and practical experience and their ability to put it across to others in an interesting manner. Inevitably, those selected for this task should be practising rifle shots with something of a personal reputation. As such, they will almost certainly be fairly fully occupied with their own personal activities throughout the target shooting season and it may prove difficult to get a team of first class instructors assembled at one place for even a short period such as a week-end. For this reason, it is considered that such courses could advantageously be held in the spring and autumn when there is less likelihood of their clashing with more important events in the shooting calendar.

It is perhaps unreasonable to expect an instructor to travel a considerable distance, probably at his own expense, to give one lecture probably lasting for only about an hour. If possible, other things being more or less equal, local residents should be approached first. If local talent is not available or suitable, the distant lecturer should be selected for his ability to talk on more than one subject, and should be given the opportunity to do so.

ORGANISING A ONE-DAY ELEMENTARY COACHING COURSE. As such a course is essentially for complete beginners, it must be assumed that they are unlikely to possess much target shooting equipment. However, those that do own rifles, telescopes or any other shooting gear, should be required to bring it with them. For the remainder, most clubs have a few rifles for general use and a few public spirited members would probably be willing to lend telescopes, ground-sheets and other similar basic essentials for such a good cause. It is suggested that a course could be run on the following lines:

Period 1. (Lecture. ¾-hour approx.) Brief ouline of technical details of rifle; how it works, effect of rifling, flight of bullet, gravity and wind effects, principles of sighting arrangements, care, cleaning and maintenance. SAFETY IN HANDLING (Bolt always open, rifle never loaded except when about to fire, check after firing, careless handling—thoughtless pointing. Safe custody of firearms and ammunition etc, see chapters 2, 3, 7 and 13).

Period 2. (Practical. 1-hour). Rifles and small targets for aiming practice. Adopting a comfortable prone position. Use of sling, correct length etc. Breathing. Assist pupils to adopt a comfortable firing position, with correct sling adjustment etc. Discuss canting, see chapters 7, 9 and 10.

Period 3. (Lecture. ¾-hour). Aiming and sight setting. Explain principles of aiming. Use of ring and blade foresights. Size of aperture. Filters, lenses and spectacles. Reading the vernier scale (Diagram required, see figure 31). This can be effectively reproduced on a blackboard if one is available, see chapters 7, 10 and 11.

Period 4. (Lecture. ¾-hour). Use of score book and general hints on shooting equipment (chapter 12).

Period 5. (Practical). Demonstration of zeroing on range. If time and facilities permit, each pupil should be given the opportunity of firing a few rounds under supervision. (chapter 7).

If the number of pupils on the course require a longer than two-hour session on the Zeroing range, there will probably be no time for further instruction. If, however, time is available, the class can be divided into two or three teams for a 'quiz' on the various subjects on which they have received instruction. If a time limit is imposed, it should be possible to ask eighteen or twenty questions in an hour, or less.

The foregoing is just a suggested programme and the detailed arrangements will have to be worked out in the light of availability of instructors, range facilities, time factor etc. It is, however recommended that the suggested general sequence be adhered to as closely as possible.

SYLLABUS FOR A WEEK-END ADVANCED COACHING COURSE. The form a more advanced course will take will again depend on the time factor and the availability of instructors etc., and the level of knowledge of those for whom it is intended. The organizers should be able to adapt it to suit their needs, and the following is an outline syllabus considered suitable for a week-end course, commencing on a Friday evening and finishing fairly early the following Sunday morning:

Friday evening (Approx. 1½- hours)
Technical aspects—theory of rifles and ammunition. Reading the vernier scale. Testing trigger pressures. Cleaning etc. The instructor will require examples of modern Target Rifles, trigger tester and, if possible, an enlarged diagram showing sight scales etc. (chapters 3, 4, 6 and 7).

Saturday morning
Period 1 (approx. ¾-hour). Grouping and zeroing—general (chapter 7).
Period 2 (approx 1½-hours). Practical demonstration of zeroing on the range, all students being given the opportunity to fire.
Period 3 (approx ¾-hour). Group centring, error chasing, canting (chapter 7).

Saturday afternoon.
Period 1 (approx ¾-hour). Keeping a score-book, including elevations, graphs etc. 'Honesty in recording'. 'Post Mortems' (chapter 12).
Period 2 (approx ¾-hour). Wind judging (chapter 11). If possible, this should take the form of a practical discussion and demonstration on the range. If there is any mirage and students have telescopes, the instructor should be able to make this very interesting and informative. Small groups are better than large ones and if the class can be divided among two or three instructors, so much the better.
Period 3 (approx ¾-hour). Optical problems. Long and short sight, Master eye etc. Lenses, spectacles, use of filters. Finding most suitable size of backsight aperture (chapters 7 and 10).

Saturday evening.
Brains Trust. If possible, all instructors should be available to answer questions. Students should have been encouraged to consider their problems and present written questions to the question-master at the commencement of the session. Impromptu questions during the session should also be encouraged.

Sunday morning.
Period 1. (approx ¾-hour). Team shooting. Selection, organization, coaching methods (chapter 14).
Period 2. Coached team shoot. This could take the form of a match between two teams of students. It is suggested that 200 and 500 yards would probably be the most suitable distances. Depending on time available and numbers involved seven or ten shots could be fired at each range. If it is necessary for the course to disperse early, the match could be completed in the morning, ten shots at only one range being fired. If time permits it would be better to fire ten shots with two sighters in the morning at 200 yards, and the same at 500 yards after lunch. This would allow more time to assist inexperienced firers. The instructors should act as team captains and wind coaches, and every opportunity should be taken of demonstrating the points made in the course of the week-end's instruction.

If range facilities are limited or if the weather is unsuitable, the use of air rifles indoors is strongly recommended. Valuable instruction and practical application can be provided in conditions that are reasonably warm and comfortable.

If the students on the course are very inexperienced it may be considered advisable to allocate time to instruction in adopting a correct and comfortable shooting position, the use of the sling and other elementary matters. This could be at the expense of the period on team shooting, and the programme would then require rearrangement in order to introduce the additional subject at Period 1 on the Saturday morning.

It would be beneficial for each student to be given an inexpensive score-book at the commencement of the course if he does not already possess one.

Target shooters generally have a good appreciation of the lethal nature of the weapons they use, and on any course of instruction, particularly when the students are beginners, the observation of safety measures both in the gunroom and on the range cannot be over-stressed.

17

THE N.R.A.—ITS INFLUENCE AT HOME AND ABROAD

The National Rifle Association was formed in 1860 and its purpose then, as now; 'To promote and encourage marksmanship throughout the Queen's Dominions in the interests of defence and the permanence of the Volunteer and Auxiliary Forces, Naval, Military and Air'.

Since its inception, the Association has played an important part in the framework of British national defence and its value to the nation, particularly in time of war, has been abundantly demonstrated. It is a registered charity with its headquarters at Bisley Camp in Surrey. It has a governing body or Council consisting of elected and ex-officio members serving on a voluntary basis. The day to day administration is carried out by a permanent salaried staff.

Close co-operation is maintained with the Ministry of Defence, the National Small-bore Rifle Association and the various governing bodies of overseas rifle associations whose conduct of rifle shooting is on similar lines. This applies to most Commonwealth countries, Rhodesia, South Africa and, to a limited extent, the United States of America.

In addition to the administration and maintenance of Bisley Camp and Ranges—in itself a major undertaking—the Association is responsible for the conduct of the Annual Prize Meeting held in July and for the continuous review and amendment of its Regulations governing competitive target shooting. These Regulations, with their attendant definitions, appendices etc., are accepted throughout the Commonwealth by rifle associations as the basis of their own rules and in fact many adhere to them as they stand with only minor amendments to suit local conditions.

The Bisley Ranges, which surround the Camp, are part of a Ministry of Defence training area and are leased to the National Rifle Association on a maintenance basis. Bisley Camp itself is the property of the Association having been acquired in 1890 when the decision was made to move from Wimbledon Common. In the Camp are numerous club-houses, privately owned huts, sleeping accommodation, stores etc. There are also considerable areas of camping sites suitable for caravans or tents. The upkeep of the ranges and the buildings owned by the N.R.A. is a heavy financial burden and in consequence it is essential that all who rely on the Association for the provision of their shooting facilities, whether directly or indirectly, should support it by becoming individual members. Similarly, clubs, associations, schools and Service units can affiliate, the fees being dependent on the size of their membership. It is through affiliation to the N.R.A. that rifle clubs are able to purchase selected quality ammunition at favourable rates—one of the most important benefits from supporting the parent organization.

Individual membership of varying categories is a condition of entry for the annual Bisley Prize Meeting. Privileges of membership include the right to hire N.R.A.-owned rifles—by the day or annually—and to buy ammuniton at favourable rates, hire target spaces on the ranges and obtain a free copy of the N.R.A. Journal as part of the subscription, and have voting rights at the Council elections and general meetings.

TARGET SHOOTING AT BISLEY—THE NATIONAL MEETING. This is held on the Bisley ranges in July and lasts for about two weeks. The programme, with a few exceptions, is open to 'all comers' and includes individual and team competitions with rifle, pistol and sporting rifle.

The first week of the Meeting is devoted to the Match Rifle and Service Rifle events. The match rifle competitions are held on Stickledown Range at distances from 900 to 1,200 yards, the principal prize being the Hopton Aggregate for the Match Rifle Championship. They conclude with the Elcho Shield international match between teams of eight from England, Scotland and Ireland. Established in 1862, the Elcho is the oldest international team event in the Bisley programme.

The Service Rifle competitions take place on the Century range at distance of 100 to 500 yards. They are designed for the armed forces, regular and auxiliary. The principal individual competitions are the Queen Mary—which includes fire with movement, rapid and snapshooting—and the Service Rifle Championship, which is the grand aggregate of the Service Rifle competitions. Concurrent with the Queen Mary is H.M. The Queen's Medal which is awarded to the best shot in the

Territorial and Army Volunteer Reserve. The principal Service rifle team match is for the United Service Challenge Cup. Open to teams of eight from the armed forces, it is fired under similar conditions to the Queen Mary.

About three days of the Meeting are largely devoted to schools cadets, culminating in the match for the Ashburton Shield. This was established in 1861, when teams of eleven from Eton, Harrow and Rugby took part. It is now open to school cadet teams of eight and about ninety schools from all parts of the United Kingdom, including the Channel Islands, participate.

The Second week of the Meeting—as far as the rifle is concerned—is all Target Rifle, and the competitions embrace all distances from 200 to 1,000 yards. The principal individual event is for H.M. The Queen's Prize, which usually attracts about a thousand competitors, including many from the Commonwealth countries. It is open only to Her Majesty's subjects and is the 'blue riband' of British target shooting. About three-hundred prizes are awarded, the first being the N.R.A. gold medal and gold badge and a cash award of £250 presented by the reigning Monarch. The contest is decided in three stages. The first comprises seven round shoots at 200, 500 and 600 yards, the highest scorer getting a bronze badge and N.R.A. bronze medal. The first three-hundred qualify for the second stage at 300, 500 and 600 yards (10 shots at each distance), the highest scorer receiving a silver badge and N.R.A. silver medal. The first hundred in this stage go forward to the Final, or 'Queen's Hundred', at 900 and 1,000 yards, each being awarded a Queen's Badge.

Next in importance are the competitions for the St. George's, the Grand Aggregate, the All-Comers Aggregate and the Duke of Gloucester's prize. The St. George's, which dates back to 1862, is also shot for in three stages. The first two are at 300 and 600 yards respectively and are eliminating stages from which the top hundred fire in the final stage at 900 yards.

During the second week, international, inter-service, and inter-county and club team contests are decided. These include the National Challenge trophy (200, 500 and 600 yards) open to the Home Countries, the Mackinnon Cup (900 and 1,000 yards) and the Kolapore Match (300, 500 and 600 yards). The last two events are open also to specified international teams from overseas.

For the period of the National Meeting, Bisley Camp is transformed into a self-contained township. The limited accommodation of the resident clubs is taxed to overflowing and the majority of the competitors are housed in huts or caravans Accommodation is booked in advance through the N.R.A.

Feeding arrangements include a well organised N.R.A. Pavilion, providing all meals and a comfortable bar-lounge. The resident rifle clubs cater for their members. Well-known firms of rifle specialists attend to the many problems and requirements of the marksmen, and shooting aids or accessories can be purchased in Bisley Camp.

As the Meeting progresses, interest in the results of the various competitions increases. So efficient is the Statistical Department of the N.R.A. that results are posted on the notice-boards shortly after the completion of each competition.

Perhaps the most outstanding feature, and one which cannot fail to impress the newcomer, is the prevailing spirit of friend-liness. While many inevitably leave at the end of a Meeting with feelings of disappointment, few depart from Bisley Camp who are not firmly resolved to come again the following year.

THE BISLEY PROGRAMME BOOK. The N.R.A. Programme Book, better known in target shooting circles as the 'Bisley Bible' is a mine of useful information. It is published annually a few months before the National Meeting and in it will be found:

1. N.R.A. rules and regulations.
2. A programme of each day's shooting with range location and time periods for each event.
3. Details of charges for the types of accommodation available for booking.
4. A map of Bisley Camp, showing the location of the ranges, club-houses, camp-sites etc.
5. Details of target dimensions, method of squadding, marking, signalling shot values, and all other matters both on and off the range with which a competitor should beome conversant.

The handbook can be purchased from the N.R.A. and is an indispensable item of equipment to a Bisley Competitor, particularly a newcomer.

THE BISLEY RANGES. The ranges at Bisley comprise the Century, with one hundred targets at distances from 100 to 600 yards; Stickledown, on which there are fifty targets at distances from 800 to 1,200 yards; and the Shorts, with thirty targets at 200 yards. To the north-east of the Century range are two further ranges, known as Short and Long Siberia.

In addition are the Sporting Rifle range (for Running Deer, Boar etc.); the Clay Bird (Bisley Gun Club); the Cheylesmore for Pistol (Silhouette targets etc.); the Pistol Gallery Range and the rifle zeroing range. Although most of the competitive target rifle shooting takes place between March and October, there is limited activity on most of the ranges all the year round.

The National Small-bore Rifle Association holds its annual National Prize Meetings at Bisley, with the rifle meeting in June and the pistol meeting during the August Bank Holiday weekend.

RANGE DUTIES AND MARKING. Since the inception of the N.R.A.'s National Meetings and up to 1967 military personnel, generally an infantry battalion augmented by detachments from the other Services, were made available by the War Office for a sufficiently long period to prepare Bisley Camp for the Meeting, to provide markers and range officials and to clear up afterwards. Since 1967 the Ministry of Defence has had to reduce its manpower assistance to the carrying out of tasks of a purely administrative nature. This has meant that competitors have been required to assist with butt-marking duties and also provide range supervisory staff.

The system of marking at Bisley by the use of coloured panels on a dual or dummy frame, is shown in figure 54 with a table below showing current target dimensions. As the target is lowered into the butts by the marker after each shot the dummy frame rises in its place, the value of the shot being indicated by a coloured panel. These panels are either black or red 'day-glow' in colour. The marker indicates the position of the shot on the target with a spotting disc and raises the target for the next shot. The dummy frame is automatically lowered at the same time. Each shot hole is patched when the spotting disc is removed; the disc having a wire stem which fits into the shot hole. Generally two or three competitiors are allocated to mark each target and consequently the work is not heavy. Since all concerned are usually thoroughly familiar with what is required, this makes for a high standard of marking.

Those appointed to perform range or butt officer duties are generally selected from the more experienced marksmen who are known to have a good working knowledge of N.R.A. rules and Regulations.

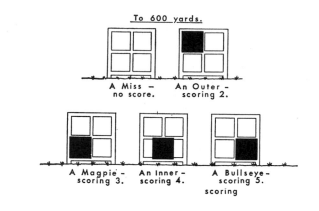

To 600 yards.

A Miss –
no score.

An Outer –
scoring 2.

A Magpie –
scoring 3.

An Inner –
scoring 4.

A Bullseye –
scoring 5.
scoring

Beyond 600 yards.

A Miss –
no score

An Outer –
scoring 2.

A Magpie –
scoring 3.

An Inner –
scoring 4.

A A Bullseye –
scoring 5.

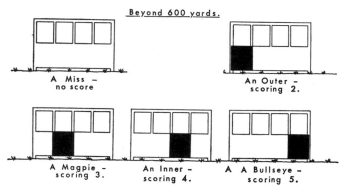

Fig. 54. The Marking System.

Target dimensions may change according to the prevailing requirements. In 1975 the following were in force for target rifle shooting in the United Kingdom.

White with circular black aiming mark.

Divisions	Diameters in inches					Scoring
	Long Range	600 yds	500 yds	300 yds	200 yds	
Aiming Mark ..	40	36	36	21	14	
Bull	24	14	11	6	3.75	5
Inner	54	27	27	13.5	9	4
Magpie ..	84	36	36	21	14	3
Outer	Rest of target 10ftx6ft	72	72	36	24	2

SAFETY. In the hands of a careless person, a rifle is an extremely dangerous weapon and safety precautions must therefore be strictly observed at all times, whether on or off the range.

The Bisley Range regulations allow a competitor to load his rifle only after he is in position on the firing-point. In no circumstances should a rifle be aimed on the ranges except from the firing position on the firing-point. The bolt should remain open at all times on the range when the rifle is not actually being fired, and it should become a matter of routine when picking up a rifle to open the bolt and ensure there is no live round in the chamber.

The rifle of every competitor at the Bisley Meeting must be inspected by or on behalf of the range officer immediately after firing at any distance. Bisley Regulations state: 'A competitor who fails to present his firearm for inspection, whether called on to do so or not, may be considered as "acting in a way that might prove dangerous" and be dealt with accordingly'.

The Regulations also state: 'A competitor acting in a dangerous manner shall forthwith be forbidden to fire again until the circumstances have been investigated and decided on by the Bisley Committee'.

The N.R.A. Journal. This is issued quarterly and is a privilege both of individual membership and corporate affiliation. Non-members are also permitted to buy it. Its aim is to keep all marksmen fully informed on all matters pertaining to their sport.

TARGET SHOOTING OVERSEAS. Target shooting is conducted in many Commonwealth countries, South Africa, Rhodesia, and to some extent in the United States on similar lines to those prevailing in the United Kingdom. The recent change in the British N.R.A. rules has to a large extent brought into line, at any rate as far as weapons and ammunition are concerned, many foreign countries with whom there has previously been little or no common ground.

Most European and many other countries confine their target shooting to the conditions laid down by the International Shooting Union, which does not include competitive shooting at ranges beyond 300 metres. Now, however, there is no reason why such countries should not visit the United Kingdom and compete under its conditions and vice versa. In recent years there have been several such exchange visits, generally arranged at rifle club level.

Opportunities for international shooting may well be improved by the standardisation of cartridge and type of rifle, which eliminates one of the former almost insurmountable obstacles to such events. While it is probable that most British marksmen, who for many years have shown a decided preference for prone position shooting in which increasing age and disabilities are not necessarily a handicap, may not take kindly to the physical strain involved in 'three-positional' shooting which is largely practiced under I.S.U. rules, undoubtedly those that start young enough and are sufficiently keen will make a success of it.

Since the formation of the National Rifle Association official teams and numerous individual overseas visitors, including a few from the United States, have visited the United Kingdom and taken part in the Bisley and other important prize meetings. During recent years, representative British teams have toured Australia, Canada, New Zealand, the West Indies, Rhodesia, South Africa, Zambia and Kenya. In addition, Oxford and Cambridge Universities have sent combined teams, and a team of school cadets (Athelings) makes annual exchange visits to Canada. There is no doubt that these visits strengthen the friendship which thrives between marksmen at home and overseas. Bisley would be a much duller place were it not for the attendance of visitors from overseas who not only give the British marksmen exciting and hard-fought competition but whose cheerful presence adds greatly to the social atmosphere prevailing at the annual prize meetings.

CANADA. The governing body is the Dominion of Canada Rifle Association, with headquarters at Ottawa. Each Province has its own Rifle Association and annual Provincial Prize Meeting. During these meetings, the competitors shoot for places in the teams to represent the Provinces at what are known as the 'Annual Rifle Matches' conducted by the D.C.R.A. and held at the Connaught Range, Ottawa. The Provincial representatives have their travelling expenses subsidised, which is an important factor when one considers the distances they have to travel to compete in what is in effect their National Prize Meeting. For instance, the distance from Vancouver Island to Ottawa is nearly as great as that travelled by the United Kingdom teams when they visit Ottawa.

The Connaught Ranges, which are the largest in Canada, are about twenty miles from the City of Ottawa. They have the unique feature of possessing two sets of targets—one at a distance of 600 yards and the other 1,000 yards—from a common firing-point. It is therefore possible to fire at all ranges from 200 to 1,000 yards with the minimum of physical exertion. As the range comprises a large number of targets which inevitably cover a wide front, this is an important consideration. The only objection to this otherwise excellent arrangement appears to be the wear and tear on some of the firing-points which are common to more than one distance.

The principal event at the annual D.C.R.A. Meeting is for the Governor-General's Prize, which is shot for in stages in much the same way as for the Queen's Prize at Bisley. The best prize list is that of the 'Bisley Aggregate', which comprises the Grand Aggregate and the final stage of the Governor-General's Prize. The top eighteen or so Canadians in the Bisley Aggregate qualify as the official D.C.R.A. team to visit the United Kingdom the following year—all expenses paid.

The chief international team events, which take place when representative teams from the United Kingdom and/or other Commonwealth countries are present, are the Canada Match (300, 500 and 600 yards) and the Commonwealth Match (900 and 1,000 yards). The Canada match trophy was presented by the Canadian National Railways for Empire competition and the Commonwealth trophy was given for the same purpose by the Canadian Pacific Railway Company.

Canada has a long target shooting history and the first Canadian team to visit the United Kingdom and take part in the Imperial Meeting at Wimbledon was sent by the Ontario Rifle Association in 1871, and fired in the first match for the Kolapore Trophy. In the N.R.A. Handbook of 1861 it is recorded that prize meetings in Canada that year were organized by the Nova Scotia Rifle Association, the New Brunswick and the Prince Edward Island Rifle Associations.

The shooting season in Canada normally extends from April to September, though this varies somewhat on account of the climatic conditions prevailing in certain localities. Obviously, where heavy falls of snow are late in melting in the spring, the commencement of the target shooting season is delayed. Similarly, unexpectedly early snowfall in the autumn will stop most shooting activities. During the month of August when the D.C.R.A. Meeting takes place, the climatic conditions are not unlike those in England—though generally there is a better chance of fine, hot weather.

AUSTRALIA. The National Rifle Association of Australia formed in 1887 as the Council of Rifle Associations of Australia, is the governing body and co-ordinates the activities of the six States, each of which has its own Association. Until 1972 there was no all-Australia National Meeting, each State having its own 'Queen's Prize'. However, with the advantages of modern travel, Australia's vast distances became less of a problem and the N.R.A. of Australia now holds its National Meeting and Queen's Prize at Canberra. This is á relatively small and new range and the number of competitors in this National Meeting is restricted to nominations from each State. Most of the main rifle meetings are held between October and April—the Australian summer—though generally speaking the climate is such that shooting can be and is conducted all the year round.

The State meetings, which in Victoria and New South Wales attract up to six-hundred competitors, are undoubtedly the best means of providing for the requirements of the majority of Australian marksmen. Competitive shooting is almost entirely civilian with few Service personnel participating. The State Queen's Prizes are not, in fact, presented by Her Majesty as in the United Kingdom, being really State Championships, all conducted on similar lines. They are open to all-comers and some marksmen tour the country and shoot in as many as possible.

As is to be expected, the weather conditions for target shooting are generally hot, with tricky, fast-changing winds. For instance, on the Williamstown Range in Victoria it is not uncommon for the wind to change direction completely—as much as 180 degrees in the course of a shoot.

Australians like to shoot fast and singly, the members of each squad taking turns at marking register cards and blackboards when competition shooting. Convertible sighting shots are permitted and the firer must declare whether or not to convert immediately upon the appearance of his target after his second sighter.

NEW ZEALAND. In New Zealand target shooting is very popular and, bearing in mind the country's relatively small population, the number of competitors who attend the various rifle meetings is considerable. The governing body is the National Rifle Association of New Zealand.

New Zealand's marksmen are outstanding where long range shooting under difficult conditions—which often prevail on their ranges—is concerned. A particularly friendly and informal spirit prevails among them. In competitive shooting the method of squadding is similar to that in Australia.

THE WEST INDIES AND OTHER ISLANDS. Rifle shooting seems to have a special appeal to island communities. This may be largely due to a deep seated feeling of preparation for defence against possible invasion. Or it may be that, surrounded by sea, no great difficulty is experienced in constructing rifle ranges, the sea being readily available to provide the requisite danger areas. Whatever the explanation, there is no doubt that the West Indian Islands of Jamaica, Trinidad and Barbados, the Falkland Islands and the Channel Islands all have tremendous enthusiasm for target shooting, and the same spirit prevails in Guyana which, though not an island, is part of the West Indies.

In all these countries, the rules and regulations of the British National Rifle Association are strictly observed and all of them are regularly represented by teams and/or individuals at the Bisley Meetings.

RHODESIA. Rhodesia has its own Rifle Association, whose rules and regulations closely follow those of the United Kingdom. More emphasis is laid on Service Rifle shooting in this country and very close liaison exists with the military and police, both forces taking a very active part in organizing and supporting competitive target shooting.

An annual Central Prize Meeting is normally held on the Cleveland Range, Salisbury, nearly 5,000 feet above sea level, although periodically it is held at Woolendale Range, Bulawayo.

SOUTH AFRICA. South Africa is endowed with all the necessities for providing a marksman's paradise. The climatic conditions are as nearly perfect as could reasonably be expected, with bright clear light, brilliant sunshine and sufficient mirage to give a true guide for judging wind strength. There are numerous ranges, some at high altitude with consequently low barometric pressure which has a beneficial effect on bullet flight. The ammunition manufactured in the country is of a high quality and the authorities look with a benevolent eye on the sport of rifle shooting. The standard of scoring is high and the South African 'shottists', as they call themselves, are justifiably proud of their marksmanship.

South African Rifle Association rules closely follow those of the United Kingdom but, as in Australia and New Zealand, convertible sighting shots are allowed.

APPENDIX

RIFLES AS PERMITTED BY THE N.R.A. AND REVISED TARGET DIMENSIONS

SERVICE RIFLE CLASS (S.R.)

The .303 in. British No. 4 Rifle manufactured by or for the British Government, or the same pattern manufactured by or for a Commonwealth Government, or of private manufacture and bearing the Government Viewer's marks.

The 7.62 mm Self-loading Rifle as issued by the British or a Commonwealth Government, and used without any un-authorised alterations or additions. The only alterations permitted are to the foresight and changing of butt.

The backsight must be as issued, with the wind-gauge, if any, set centrally. The foresight must be a blade, which may be undercut.

Rifles must be fitted with a safety catch and magazine, and stocking-up must be in accordance with *Ministry of Defence regulations*, full details of which can be found in the N.R.A. Programme Book.

TARGET RIFLE CLASS (T.R.)

Any rifle as defined for S.R. and any bolt-actioned rifle which, in the opinion of the N.R.A. Council, is of conventional design. This is intended to include any military design of bolt-action rifle, British or Foreign, and privately made versions of these designs.

The complete rifle, or all its components, must be readily available in quantity and must not exceed 5.25 kg (11.64 lb.) in weight, excluding sling.

The barrel must be suitable for firing the 7.62 mm NATO cartridge or the .303 in. Mark 7 cartridge.

Full details of rifles which conform to the foregoing and which are in use in target shooting, and methods of stocking-up, are given in chapters three and four.

MATCH RIFLE CLASS (M.R.)

Any rifle with a 7.62 mm barrel and of a maximum weight of $5\frac{1}{2}$ lb. Sights may be any, including magnifying or telescope, and a rubber butt plate or shoe may be fitted. Minimum trigger pull—1.5 kg (3.3 lb.).

INDEX